Firecrackers

Firecrackers

The Exploits of an Expat in China

Anna Keibler

Apprentice
House Press
Loyola University Maryland

First Edition

Library of Congress Control Number: 2025949825

Hardcover ISBN: 978-1-62720-644-0
Paperback ISBN: 978-1-62720-645-7
Ebook ISBN: 978-1-62720-646-4

Design by Apprentice House Press
Editorial Development & Design Editing by Aminah Murray
Promotional Development by Nick Kelly

Published by Apprentice House Press

Apprentice
House Press
Loyola University Maryland

Loyola University Maryland
4501 N. Charles Street, Baltimore, MD 21210
410.617.5265
www.ApprenticeHouse.com / info@ApprenticeHouse.com

Contents

Introduction vii

When We Were Naked 1

New Year, Old Firecracker 19

So You Think You're a Teacher? 45

The Foreign Haze 67

What Happened in Qingdao 87

No Turkeys in China 95

A Taste of Failure 103

Lisa's Game 111

Are We Part of a Scandal? 113

It's Hard to Make Hamburgers 139

I Think I Need a Doctor 151

If You Can't Stand the Heat 177

Love in the Time of WiFi: The True Love Network 181

About the Author 209

Introduction

In 2011, at the ripe age of nineteen years old, I traveled from my hometown in southern Indiana, with a population of just under 1,000 residents, to the Tier-2 city of Jinan, the capital city of Shandong, China. Jinan was considered a small city, despite its seven million residents, and was renown for its dozens of artesian wells and springs that bespeckled the city. I originally ventured to the Middle Kingdom as a foreign exchange student and intended to only stay for a semester. However, I fell in love with this city and stayed wrapped in its embrace until 2016.

When I arrived at Shandong University I discovered I was the only American among 300 people housed in the foreign student dorms. We came from everywhere… stand in front of a map, close your eyes, and jab your finger on a random country. Whatever country you land on, at least one student called it home. With so many mingling cultures, expectations, and desires to be free, we created our own unique culture within our expat communities, a conglomerate of social rules pulled from this custom and that custom, mingling our morals and views on society until we all found a happy medium within ourselves.

We were young and living fiercely. We drank, smoked, danced, and took drugs like it was nobody's business, making deep connections with like-minded local residents along the way. I can't say I'm particularly proud of everything I did in China, but it sure was one helluva adventure, and I long for the vibrant community we created for ourselves.

The following stories are all true, although some names and situations have been changed for privacy, but each story is told as remembered. Some of these stories have even become expat lore, still whispered around the city after more than a decade. Those of us who stayed in China long-term went to great measures to integrate ourselves into Chinese society, but we were still drawn to the we're-all-in-this-together family dynamic among the expats. It is possible to live in both worlds, with one foot fully planted in living a wild adventure and the other planted in The Chinese Dream. Sometimes, the two even went hand-in-hand. I hope you enjoy reading these stories as much as I enjoyed living them.

When We Were Naked

In an attempt to cleanse the sweat from my overweight, nineteen-year-old body during the muggy summer air and integrate more with the expat community, I began skinny dipping in a local literal watering hole called the Black Tiger Spring. It was 2012 when a group of English teachers from Aston English Training School showed me their favorite place for a nightly swim—one of the few sources of freshwater in the city. I'd always been drawn to water. I could look at rain puddles and feel compelled to dive in. So, having access to a place to swim in the city, especially in a place so beautiful and refreshing, felt like a divine gift. I didn't care that my clothes were soaked. I didn't care that the water was cold enough to give me goosebumps. I was just happy to feel like I was a part of nature again, as well as a part of this new group of people I was trying desperately to break into.

Jinan was known as the "City of Springs", and my heart was pulled to the hundreds of artesian wells that sprang up from under the city center, teeming with koi fish the city nurtured and minnows that nature sustained. The second-most-famous of these springs was named Black Tiger Spring, where our little pool was located, which sat inside Huancheng park. Just outside the city center, perfectly manicured flora rose up in between detailed stone carvings and ornate wooden pavilions throughout the park, and the winding paths became a favorite destination for us inebriated foreigners.

Concrete blocks sectioned off the little pool from the DongLuo river, forming an elevated ten-foot-by-twelve-foot basin. When it wasn't full of naked night owls, the pool was easily accessible to the elderly, and just before daybreak, one could witness a steady stream of old men and women lining up to refill their recycled two-gallon sunflower oil jugs with clean spring water. Some would even drink the water straight, no boiling or filtering. I was never brave enough to try. The first time I tagged along after a night out, six of us all jumped in together, letting the almost unnaturally clean water envelop our hot and sticky summer bodies. I was surprised at how deep the pool was. Standing at five-foot-two, I could barely reach the bottom with my tippy toes.

At night, the pool was empty, especially on the Sunday and Monday nights that constituted the typical English teacher's weekend. The elderly were all in bed, and most locals didn't swim. Still, the odd Jinaner or two could occasionally be found relaxing in the cool waters, usually either well on their way to getting drunk or completely toked. The Aston teachers had taken a page from this playbook and decided that joining this extracurricular activity would make for a grand night. They weren't wrong.

Despite the late hour—nearing on 2:00 am—the area was well lit. A bright blue streetlamp illuminated the spring, making the water dance and sparkle. Of course, it also ensured that none of us inadvertently stumbled into the water. The park was mostly empty, save for a few late-night power walkers and lovers-in-arms seeking sanctuary beneath the trees. Occasionally, someone would stop and talk with us, curious about the group of slightly rowdy foreigners in the water. We tried to get them to join us, but nobody took us up on the offer. They were happy to sit with us for a moment, though, listening to our stories spoken in broken Chinese.

Shortly afterwards, with our case of beer empty, we dragged our pruned bodies out of the spring and back onto dry land, dripping puddles onto the cobblestone pathways. We dutifully discarded our trash in the nearest trash can (people in Jinan were more likely to leave their trash behind, as they viewed waste management to be the job of street sweepers) and traversed out of the park to the main road. As we went our separate ways for the evening, I hailed a taxi. I was still incredibly damp. I wasn't dripping, but my wet shorts were enough for the taxi driver to look utterly displeased with me.

"You're all wet!" he cried. "What have you been doing? Some mischief, maybe?"

"I went swimming in the spring back there," I replied, smiling.

The driver let out a hard "huh" noise, and rolled down the windows, surely hoping that the breeze would dry me off a bit and save his seats from getting soaked.

"Would you like a cigarette?" I asked, pulling out my pack of Yuxi's. They were an expensive brand with a bold flavor not for the weak of heart.

I watched a grin creep across his face. "Thanks," he said. "I really like these."

I stuck my lighter out between the metal bars that separated the driver and passenger seats. He leaned down into the flame, trying to keep one eye on the road, and tapped my hand when he was done. It was the least I could do, considering the wet butt print I'd be leaving behind. We had the typical conversation on the drive back to my apartment.

"Where are you from?"

Indiana, in America.

"What are you doing in Jinan?"

Teaching English and studying Chinese. Yes, it keeps me very busy.

"How is your Chinese so good?"

I've been studying for a long time, but I still make a lot of mistakes.

"Were you born with that hair?"

No, but it is *really my hair.*

"Do you want to be my QQ friend?"

Absolutely.

I always agreed to be their QQ friend. I was fairly enamored by the social media site and had collected dozens of once-met acquaintances with whom to practice my Chinese, occasionally meeting up for a coffee or dinner as the token foreigner.

When the driver reached my apartment complex, he turned to me and said, "I don't like that you got my car wet… but I *am* glad that you're enjoying the springs."

"Thank you, sir," I replied quite formally. "I can't wait to get out of these clothes."

From then on, I visited Black Tiger Springs at least once a week, always after the bars were closed, and usually with a bottle of vodka in hand. The group of friends I went with varied. Sometimes, I would make my university friends or coworkers tag along, too, mixing my social groups to create a more cohesive expat experience (something I would be chastised for the following year.) But it only took a few more swims before we all realized that it was exceedingly inconvenient to get our clothes wet.

Most of us didn't even own a bathing suit in China, and even if we did, our routine was to gather downtown straight after the workday ended, no time to go home and grab swimming gear. Sure, we *could* swim with our clothes on, but the spring was miles from our apartments, and taxi drivers were loath to give a ride to someone soaking wet. Even further, drying out in the muggy summer heat took hours, and we didn't want to wait around until sunrise before getting home.

So, the logical conclusion was to just avoid getting our clothes wet altogether, and we began to skinny dip. I had absolutely zero qualms about being naked in front of other people. Since I was fat, I didn't consider myself attractive, and instead of being ashamed and trying to hide my body, I decided to use my fatness as a shield. I was already hearing, "Look, she's so fat!" every day on the street from the mouths of strangers who thought I couldn't speak the language. Nobody in our group was sexually attracted to me, and if they didn't want to look at my fat body that bobbed joyfully in the water, they could look at my eyes instead.

The first time we jumped naked into the pool, our group was comprised of two gay men, two straight men, and three straight women. The other women and gay men didn't care about seeing one another's bodies, but the two straight guys took a bit of coaxing. Go figure. Still, it was a delightful swim that solidified our actions as a new trend.

Skinny dipping in the springs was the best way to gauge who my real friends were. When I was with the group that originally introduced me to the pool, I always felt a little sidelined. Nobody *really* wanted to listen when I tried to start a conversation, and very few people would look me in the eyes while they talked, instead opting to look past me or turn their heads to the side when they responded to my comments and questions. Thankfully, other people were incredibly happy to have me in their company, asking me directly to join them in the spring, playing with me and jesting with me and sharing their cigarettes, truly wanting to form those bonds of friendship. Soon, the two groups separated, with the teachers I tried so hard to get to like me off on their own private escapades as the novelty of the springs had worn off, and the rest of us continuing the weekend tradition.

This new crew that formed – *our* crew – included those with a taste for the weird, queer, and extreme. We loved dirty jokes. We loved befriending strangers. We saw romance underneath the filth of the city. We were *hungry*. Not for food, but for adventure, and Jinan was ours for the taking. Except, as we sometimes forgot, we were far from the only people in Jinan, and in a city of 7 million, there were no secret hideouts.

One night, as we skipped arm-in-arm to the spring, we found the pool full of locals. They weren't naked, unfortunately, but they were drinking beer and baijiu—China's signature grain alcohol—and smoking cigarettes and having the time of their lives, just like we planned to do. I remember feeling disappointed at first, but soon perked up as Matt, a gay British man in his mid-twenties who'd been in China for years (and was the perfect leader of our crew), nudged me in the ribs and said, "I bet we could join them."

We approached with our "ni hao's" and hand waves, spoke the best Mandarin we could muster, and asked if they didn't mind making a few foreign friends. But they did mind. They wanted no part of us there.

"No," said the largest bloke. Just that one English word.

We were a little shocked. Jinan was renowned for being so friendly and laid back, as opposed to "rude" Beijing or "sly" Shanghai, but what could we do? We certainly couldn't crash their party, and we had nowhere else to swim. Feeling sorry for ourselves, we headed to the Muslim Quarter a few blocks away for the all-night goat and garlic barbeque skewers to drown our sorrows in as much meat and weak beer as possible. We would try to swim again the next night.

But sure enough, as we approached the pool the next night after 2:00 a.m., we found it already occupied—not by the same people, but by three older women. Dressed in their bathing suits and speaking in *Jinan Hua* (the local Jinan dialect), they were hard at work scrubbing their bodies and filling the spring with soapy bubbles. We felt it would be disrespectful to disturb them, so we tucked our disappointed tails between our legs and went back to our apartments. Perhaps next weekend?

I waited in silent anticipation for the next Sunday night to roll around. Since I worked at a different English school than most of my friends, it took a lot of work to see each other face-to-face on weekdays. Of course, we were all in the same WeChat groups and were in constant communication, sending the latest custom GIFs well before Western social media caught on to the trend. Still, it wasn't the same as being physically present.

We all met at the local Belgium restaurant, our weekly tradition, and consumed our fair share of pizza, meat, beer, and cigarettes before hopping away to our favorite bar. As the night drew to a close, we helped Wuzi, the owner, gather up the beer glasses the other patrons had left on the tables. We spent enough time there to grow rather close with Wuzi and his bartenders, to the point where we all just wanted to see him smile. Cleaning was the best way to elicit that response.

"Are you swimming tonight, Anna?" Wuzi asked.

I nodded. "Absolutely. Or at least we'll try to. We haven't been so lucky these past few times, though. Do you guys wanna come with? We can wait for you!"

Wuzi let out a hearty laugh. "No, no, I like to swim somewhere else, and never without my wife's permission."

It wasn't that his wife didn't like nude foreigners, just that she wanted her husband home at a reasonable hour for a bar owner. Of course, we understood.

Wuzi walked behind the mahogany bar and motioned me over. I watched as he stood on his tippy-toes, reaching for an unopened bottle of vodka.

"Here, take this with you. It'll almost be like I'm there," he said with a wink.

"Mmm, vanilla flavor—my favorite! Thank you, friend."

"Stop with the thank-you's. We don't say thank you to friends." He gave my back a slap as he reemerged from behind the bar, thrusting the bottle into my hands.

I held up the bottle in delight, and my friends gave a cheer. Wuzi smiled as he lit a cigarette and watched us all shuffle away.

There were five of us that night, two lads and three lasses, and as we rounded the corner of the park to the spring, we again let out a heavy sigh as we found the pool occupied. Apparently, we really had started a trend, and everyone wanted to be part of the adventure. Unfortunately, it looked like that meant no more adventuring for *us*. But just before we gave up on the night, Jameson, a half-Chinese-half-Japanese California native, turned to Matt and hollered.

"Matt! We can go to the rocks!"

"Oh!" Matt cried in response. "Yes, we have the solution!" He thrust a finger in the air with a snap.

"Come on, guys," Jameson urged as he began walking north, pushing Matt ahead of him. "You've gotta check this out!"

We followed behind closely, the other women and I jesting that this was how body parts get stolen. Sure, just follow you down this little dark path! Surely, nothing is amiss! This part of the park wasn't well-lit, with dull street lamps spaced too far apart. Luckily, the summer sky was unusually clear, and the moon was bright and full, its light reflecting off the wet cobblestones as we walked. We stopped under a wooden pavilion.

"There," Matt said, pointing out to the middle of the Dongluo River.

The river was only forty-feet across and ran rather shallow, but the water was always crystal clear and glistened in the moonlight. In the middle of the river sat a large and unassuming oval shaped pile of rocks.

"Guys, I know it looks like just a big pile of rocks, but there's actually a really deep well in there," he explained, "and all we have to do is climb up and jump in!"

"How did you guys find this?" I asked in amazement. "And *when* did you find it?"

"We were drinking earlier in the week and wanted to swim," Jameson said, "but the other spring was too crowded, so—"

"So we decided to swim in the river," laughed Matt, "and this is what we found!"

I watched as Matt fumbled trying to take his shirt off. Were we too drunk for this? No matter, this was something new! By the time I had my shoes off, Jameson was completely naked and standing on the rocky riverbank. We ladies always took our time disrobing, folding up our outfits and hiding our bras and underwear under our shirts.

Getting to the rock formation meant first getting into the river itself. Luckily, Matt and Jameson had previously found a small outcrop that provided natural steps down into the water. It was a good four-foot drop from the bank to the river, with nothing but rocks to catch you if you fell. I held on to the embankment as I followed my friends, last in line, nervous about slipping and hurting my flabby belly. The riverbed was covered in slick, sharp stones that poked into our feet as we waded across the waist-high water. I watched the group scamper up the side of the rock formation—about a five-foot climb—before finding my own footholds. I sucked in sharply as I felt a rock dislodge, and my foot slipped on the slick limestone.

"Come here, Anna," Matt said sweetly as he reached a hand down, his chest pressed firmly against the formation. "I've got you."

The inside of the rock formation was comprised of a fifteen-foot-long span of water, shallow enough to sit down in at first, and gradually growing deeper until the rocks suddenly gave way to a deep, deep well about 8 feet across. This was the source of another artesian spring, and it bubbled and churned cold water from the depths of the karst below us.

"It's at least twenty feet to the bottom," Jameson said, pointing to the well. "I can't even touch the bottom, and I'm good at diving." As an avid surfer, it was true that Jameson felt most at home in the water.

"I bet I can reach it," bragged Katherine, who was not only a coworker, but also a close friend.

"I'd like to see you try," laughed Callie, who was also a coworker and close friend. Katherine, Callie, and I were inseparable at this point.

Katherine handed the bottle of vodka to Callie, waded trepidiatiously to the well's drop-off point, drew up her hands, and dove into the water. Down and down she swam, deep into the darkness where surely no light could penetrate. We all held our breath.

"What if she hit her head?" I thought to myself, suddenly concerned that we were drinking and swimming around near sharp rocks. "What if she drowns?!"

But just as I finished my thought, Katherine's head popped back up on the far side of the well. She was grinning ear to ear, looking around to try and find us in the moonlight, slightly disoriented.

"Did you touch it?" yelled Jameson.

"I think so!" Katherine called back. "I sure touched *something!*"

"Okay, I'm getting in next," I said, and stood up from my seat in the shallow end of the oval. I wasn't a very good swimmer, so I knew I wouldn't touch the bottom, but I wanted to tread water over the deep abyss. I felt for the edge of the well with my toes, gripping at pebbles that moved under my feet. When I finally found the ledge, I took a deep breath, crouched down until my chin was level with the water, and pushed off with my feet, arms extended in front of me.

I let out a loud gasp as I glided through the water. It was so cold! The water in the shallow end was slightly chilled, but nothing like what flowed up from the well. I laughed and sputtered as I made my way around the entirety of the well, cold water finding every crevice of my body. Callie made an attempt to dive to the bottom as well, but came up quickly and screamed about the chill.

"Vodka," Matt reminded us, "that'll warm you up!"

And so the rock pool became our new weekend ritual. Matt and I were always down for a swim, and as the summer brought new foreigners into the country and the foreign university students mingled with us teachers, we had a new batch of friends to share the experience with every Sunday night. Not everyone took their clothes off, but most found bravery behind the cover of darkness and the fearlessness that alcohol inspired in us. We joked about our nudity – it was an unspoken rule not to sexualize your friends while skinny dipping, save for the night we played "rate my boobs" and "rate my cock", still all in jest.

In one instance, a new teacher found himself half-hard, staring at the naked body of a close university friend. She wasn't having any of him, though, and laughed out loud when she saw that the water he was standing in was at the same height level as his hard-on. "It's like a boat!" she hollered in amusement, and the group of us burst into laughter. He blushed deeply and proclaimed that he was too drunk to keep his body under control. That wasn't the last time he swam nude with us, but it was certainly the last time he set his boat out sailing.

One night, deep in the heart of July, we waded out to the rock pool and found it already occupied. Two Jinan men were sitting low in the shallow end, bottles of beer resting on the rocks. It was dark enough that night, we didn't see them until we were scaling up the side of the rock pile ourselves. Matt plopped into the water beside one of the men, cried out, "Ni hao!" and waved emphatically. The men both turned towards us and watched us scamper into the water, grinning wide. It took us only moments to realize that they were nude, too, and they were all smiles.

There were six of us that night, and the range of our Mandarin skills varied from knowing only how to say "hello" to being able to keep up with a quick-paced conversation. Matt and I belonged to the latter category, and we began making conversation. We introduced ourselves and offered up our vodka. But the man I was speaking to was slurring his words heavily. He waved his hands in front of him with every sentence, making strange gestures with his fingers. I looked to the second man and Matt for help, but they were deep in conversation with two other friends. Still looking at Matt, I asked the man in front of me a question. He didn't respond. When I turned my head back to face him, he gave a wide smile, turned to the rocks behind him, and grabbed a pack of cigarettes. He took two from the pack, handing one to me, grunting happily as he held out his lighter for me to use. "Thank you," I told him, matching his wide smile. His smile grew even bigger, and he replied with a slurred and muffled "you're welcome".

He tapped Matt on the shoulder, offering him a cigarette as well. Matt accepted gratefully, and turned to make conversation. The man watched Matt's face intently, and Matt also had difficulty understanding the man who gestured with his hands and fingers. Suddenly, I saw Matt's face freeze as though a lightbulb had gone off in his head.

"May I ask you," he said to the man, "are you deaf?"

The man opened his mouth and laughed, nodding his head up and down, and clapped for Matt. He wasn't drunk and slurring his words, he was speaking with a deaf accent! He wasn't waving his hands around, he was signing! And he star4ed so intently because he was reading our lips! It suddenly all made sense, and I felt a bit of a fool for not picking up on it earlier. The deaf man's friend scooted over to join us, receiving a tap on the shoulder from his friend. They signed to each other, then turned back to Matt and me.

"He wants to tell you that his name is Da Wang," his friend said, "and wants to know your names, too. I'm Xiao Ping, by the way."

Da Wang was full of questions, and Xiao Ping was more than happy to interpret between the lot of us. Da Wang was the first deaf person I'd met in China, and I was just as excited to learn from him as he was to be surrounded by naked foreigners.

"He says he loves being naked," Xiao Ping said as Da Wang signed.

"How do you sign the word for naked?" I asked. I had to

learn! Da Wang took my hands and positioned my fingers into a sign, moving my hand in the proper motion. I was delighted. "Can you teach us more?"

The eight of us sat around the rock pool that night teaching each other signs. We came from four different countries, and each of us foreigners knew a few random signs we'd picked up from school. I taught the signs for "tree", "bullshit", and "more beer, thank you". A Scottish friend knew the signs for "baby", "fuck", and "water". Da Wang was delighted. He taught us how to sign the things around us first, "beer", "swim", "cigarette", "friend", then all the curse words he could think of, correcting our fingers when we got it wrong and clapping when we got it right. An hour before sunrise, Da Wang signed that he was cold and tired and ready to go home. We thanked him and Xiao Ping for the time they spent with us, and told them we hoped to see them swimming there again in the future. Unfortunately, with our phones tucked away back at the pavilion, we were without the opportunity to exchange contact information, and we never saw the pair of friends again.

It wasn't long before our little rock pool garnered the attention of other night swimmers, just as the first pool had. It felt like every other weekend, we would venture to the rock formation, only to find it already occupied. Sometimes, we would join. Sometimes, others would join us. Some came in bathing suits, some in their street clothes, and some completely nude, but nobody was unfriendly towards us this time. Occasionally, one of our foreign friends would voice their resentment towards "our spot" being taken, and while it was disappointing to not have a secret hideout anymore, we had to remind each other that, again, in a city of 7 million people, there's no such thing as a secret hideout. But the local government wasn't fond of this new nightly skinny-dipping trend that had arisen in the city, and erected a large "NO SWIMMING" sign in front of the access point.

We found ourselves staring at the sign one night, completely in shock. What should we do? We decided to completely disregard the sign. There was nobody around in the middle of the night. Gripping a vodka bottle tight in my left hand, I held onto the sign with my right hand to steady myself on the slippery rocks of the water's edge. I was always afraid of slipping on these rocks while naked. Climbing up the embankment of the rock pool, I gently tossed the vodka bottle into the well. It floated. The bottles always floated.

We took turns treading water in the well, swimming after the vodka bottle as it floated around the pool. There were only four of us that night, and the atmosphere was relaxed. We passed around a pack of cigarettes someone had ferried over, and as soon as I struck the lighter, a blinding yellow light hit me in the eyes.

"HEY!" someone shouted. "What are you doing in there? Get out right now!"

It was a police officer! We froze as he swept his flashlight across the lot of us, hollering, "quickly, quickly!" We shuffled down from the rock pool, leaving our vodka bottle behind, and waded back across the channel.

"What are we going to do?" one of my friends whispered as reached the access point. "I can't go to jail!"

"We're not going to go to jail," hissed another friend, "but they might tell our employers!"

"Anna, get us out of this..." they turned to me, knowing that I spoke the language better than all of them combined.

My heart was pounding as I climbed back up the access point, gripping the "NO SWIMMING" sign once more for balance. I sobered up quickly, and told my friends it was highly unlikely anyone would be going to jail tonight. Maybe a fine for the violation… but then again, I'd never been *caught* breaking a law in China before, so I let my mind wonder about all the potentially terrible possibilities. Forced labor! Forced deportation! Forced to leave the vodka bottle behind in the well!

"You all, line up against the wall," the officer told us sternly as he pointed to the stones behind us. Then he made a quick flapping motion with the tips of his fingers to let us know he was serious. We tried to grab our clothes first.

"No!" he shouted. "I said up against the wall!"

We complied, and stood, backs as straight as drunkenly possible, shivering as a summer breeze rolled through, cooling the little streams of water trickling down our bodies. I said nothing to the officer, knowing that I was the default liaison, but not daring to speak without being asked a question. The officer pulled out his radio.

"I have four people here… they were swimming in Black Tiger Spring… naked," he said into the radio as he looked us over. He glanced back at the "NO SWIMMING" sign, then looked us over once more.

"Who are they?" the officer's superior's voice broke through the radio static.

"They're… they're foreigners," the officer replied, and he began to pace.

There was nothing but silence from the other end. Time seemed to slow to a crawl as it passed.

One minute.

Two minutes.

Five minutes.

And then a response…

"Just let them go," the superior replied, and we heard him

sigh over the radio.

The officer in front of us sighed, too, and motioned us towards our clothes.

"Get dressed," he said, "and then get out of here." Again, he flapped his hand in the direction of our clothes. We wasted no time rushing over to dress ourselves again, and as we did, the officer banged his flashlight against the sign.

"No swimming!" he said in English, then continued in Chinese, "this sign says it plain as day. Aiya!"

Our clothes clung tightly to our wet skin as we finished slipping on our shoes. We all knew we'd gotten lucky. Very lucky. The police simply didn't want to deal with foreigners. We meant a lot of unnecessary paperwork and translating and time and… well, we weren't actually hurting anyone or anything. But we also knew it was very unlikely we could get away with this again. Our faces were easy to remember, and the officer was obviously tasked with patrolling for "uncivilized behavior" that went against Xi JinPing's vision of the Chinese Dream – *strong China, civilized China, harmonious China, and beautiful China.*

We made sure word circulated quickly within the expat community about the no swimming policy at the Black Tiger Springs. Maybe they would let one group of foreigners go, but others might not be so lucky. It was hard to say goodbye to our tradition. We mourned our loss. We still took the occasional swim, but the next best swimming spot was a mile downstream in the DongLuo River, was very well lit, and most people couldn't touch the bottom. Once or twice we swam in DaMing Lake, which sat in the center of the city. But neither option carried the same mystique and excitement as our little rock pool with the well in the center. We closed that chapter of expat lore, leaving the tales to be passed down to the next generation of foreigners.

New Year, Old Firecracker

Just past nightfall, I exited the shopping center, clutching a new pair of stiff winter boots and the thickest fleece-lined leggings I'd ever found. A dozen bystanders had gathered on the sidewalk in front of the vendor's mall. Cell phones were pulled out, ready to record. Children held tightly to their mother's hands, eagerly jumping and pointing. I found a gap between a group of two families and sat my bags down, wondering what all the commotion was about. I realized, then, that it would be a minute before I'd be able to go any further. In fact, I thought to myself, maybe I should back up a bit.

In front of us, two men were laying out a fifty-foot-long roll of firecrackers. Cigarettes held tightly at the edges of their lips, one man was responsible for unrolling the giant spool of fireworks while the other man made sure everything laid straight. The latter also took on the responsibility of yelling warnings out to passers-by. "Wait a minute! Wait a minute!" he called out as more shoppers exited, oblivious to what was about to take place.

With all fifty feet of firecrackers laid out before them, the first man took out a lighter and knelt down at the beginning of the strand. I heard the fuse sizzle as his fire touched the fibers, and I stepped back a few paces, abandoning my bags on the sidewalk. I placed my hands over my ears and watched the two men run quickly back to the crowd.

BANG! BANG! BANG! BANG! BANG! The sound was

19

ear-splitting. BANG! BANG! BANG! Red firecracker papers were flying off into the air and floating down around us. BANG! BANG! BANG! BANG! BANG! Would it ever end? The roll was only half depleted by now and smoke was filling the air. But it continued on. BANG! BANG! BANG! And more. And more! Until finally, silence fell across the crowd as the last firecracker exploded and we watched the smoke dissipate into the street.

The two men shook hands and laughed as the people in the crowd went on their way. The remnants of the firecrackers were left on the sidewalk for the street sweepers to deal with. That was their job after all, to pick up trash in the road. And if people stopped leaving trash for them to pick up, then they wouldn't have a job anymore. So, it was okay to leave refuse lying around. At least, that was the logic my local friends had told me several times. A thin piece of red firecracker paper floated up and stuck in my hair, but with my hands full of bags, I chose to just let it be. This wasn't the first time I'd had firecracker paper cling to me, and it surely wouldn't be the last.

I was eagerly awaiting the start of the Spring Festival, or the Chinese New Year as it was called by outsiders, a fifteen-day long celebration to mark the start of the lunar year. The timing of the Spring Festival varies according to the solar calendar, starting sometime between late January and late February, culminating with the Lantern Festival on the arrival of the full moon. But celebrations typically lasted a month, starting two weeks before the actual festival. Residents bathed the city in red as they hung traditional paper cuttings and banners and shot firecrackers off in the early morning hours to greet each new day. The expat community often joked that this was the Month of War, where at any given time of day or night, you could hear what sounded like artillery fire outside your window and in the distance, all across the city. As the days leading up to the new year approached, the war sounds got worse, and many Middle Eastern friends who had come from areas prone to fighting frequently commented that they couldn't tell the difference between the firecrackers and high-powered gunfire.

During the Spring Festival everybody left the city. Our local friends and migrant friends alike all traveled back to their families' villages. For some, especially the migrant workers across the entirety of China, this was the only opportunity to go home for the entire year, and their families expected them to bring back money, clothes, and food. Travel felt impossible this time of year. Trains were always booked full, with even standing-only tickets hard to come by. Plane tickets were sold out months in advance. Most taxi drivers took vacation too, and since the buses were all on alternate schedules, it became almost impossible to get from one side of town to the other. Most of my foreign friends chose to leave the city during the Spring Festival as well, taking the opportunity to travel to warmer nearby countries like Thailand and the Philippines.

During my first year in China, I stayed behind in Jinan for the 2012 New Year. I remember walking through the once-bustling campus of Shandong University and encountering precisely zero other human beings, the large six-foot wind chimes gently clanging in the breeze. It felt like a scene from an apocalypse movie, as the silence rang just as loud as the firecrackers outside the campus walls. Luckily, a few foreign friends had stayed behind in the international student dorms and adjoining foreign teacher dorms. We clung to each other for the month, desperate for company.

By this time, I had left the university and was teaching SAT prep in the neighboring city of Tai'an, where my boss rented an apartment for me. I still kept a small studio apartment in Jinan, however, since I returned to the city on weekends. I missed living at the dorms, but I planned to only be in Tai'an for one full year before returning to my studies. My residence permit was registered in Jinan anyway, and I needed a place to store all my belongings. Unfortunately, my boss had also been withholding my paychecks, giving me just enough to barely survive until the next month rolled around, claiming that he needed that money to fund my new (illegal) visa. He needed to keep me in the country until the semester was over, and greasing the palms of a few higher ups was the cheapest route to go. Taking my paycheck was convenient for *him*, but for me, this was the poorest I'd ever been.

Living on ten yuan per day, or less than two USD, I would make my way each morning from my apartment on the thirteenth floor of a high-rise above a vendor's mall to a small cigarette cart just down the street. There, I would buy the cheapest pack of cigarettes available. Then, I would cross the street and buy two street food items, the same ones every day: a fried spinach and egg patty with an egg yolk in the center and a fried carrot patty, also sporting a yolk in the center. Then I would cross the street again to buy a liter of bottled water before making my way back to my apartment.

The cigarettes burned quickly, so I paid great attention to each one I smoked. I would smoke one before breakfast, eating a whole patty and drinking a fourth of the water. When I was finished, I would smoke another cigarette. Lunch was two more cigarettes and half of the second patty. Dinner was the same as lunch, and the remaining cigarettes were smoked throughout the day to help keep the hunger at bay. This worked, for the most part, as I never got tired of the fried egg patties, and the cigarettes—despite being cheap—were smooth in flavor.

My apartment also lacked electricity, gas, and heating, which meant I couldn't turn on the lights when it fell dark, heat up the water in the bathroom tank for a shower, or cook using the stove. And my radiator acted as a glorified shelf, since I'd never paid for my heat to be turned on. I took cold showers and brushed my teeth in darkness. I washed my clothes in cold water, too, and the cold air meant they took a long time to dry. To keep myself entertained, I charged my laptop and cell phone at the local McDonald's each day and watched the same three episodes of Six Feet Under and the same two seasons of Squidbillies on repeat.

My friends didn't know how poorly I was doing. I never told them and I don't think any of them noticed. Well, the university students didn't notice, but the older teachers and career-based expats had an idea. They could see right through my façade of "everything's okay". Angelika, a German woman in her mid-thirties, had become one of my best friends, and often sought out my company when I least expected it, inviting me for drinks and meals and funding my nights out on the town so I could at least be social. The other foreigners lovingly called her "mama", as she seemed to take care of everyone.

Five days into the Spring Festival, Angelika texted me.

"What are you doing tonight, Anna?" she asked.

That night, I'd entertained myself by sitting at my window and watching a small group that had gathered thirteen stories below. They'd brought huge boxes of professional-grade fireworks, and they were setting off the explosives right in the center of the apartment complex's courtyard. The fireworks shot up in a stream of color, bursting only a few stories higher than my apartment. I sat in awe as I watched the flames sizzle in the night sky, falling and fading at eye level. I told Angelika all about it.

"That sounds great. Can I come, too?" her text read.

Having Angelika with me sounded like the greatest pleasure I could imagine, and I told her as much, texting her the address. But I needed to get dressed… I was wearing yesterday's clothes, and I stank. I'd done laundry the day before, but none of my clothes were dry yet, and my closet was bare. I gulped and sighed, knowing what I'd have to do. I felt my long-sleeved shirts. They were all very damp. I tried my short-sleeved shirts next, and found a t-shirt that was drier than any other article of clothing. Still, the cold, wet shirt bit into my skin as I pulled it over my head and wriggled it onto my body, moisture clinging to my skin and pulling the shirt tight. I shivered, but I was hoping that my body heat would help dry the shirt before Angelika arrived.

It didn't. When Angelika texted that she was in my courtyard, the only thing I could do was throw on my winter jacket and hope the cold dampness would turn to warm dampness under my coat. I took the elevator down and met Angelika on the steps near a terrace.

"I brought wine!" she exclaimed, holding up a bottle of ChangYu red.

"Great!" I said, matching her enthusiasm. "But I don't have any cups! Or a wine opener, for that matter…"

"Don't worry about that," she said, and produced a cheap plastic wine bottle opener from her large flannel coat pocket. "As for the cups, we'll just drink from the bottle."

She opened the bottle and handed it to me for the first sip. I thanked her and let the liquor warm my mouth and tongue as I drank. Then I handed it back to Angelika, and she did the same. The fireworks boomed above, and we watched as colors rained down all around us.

"We should lay on the steps and watch," I suggested, finding the lowest step and sitting down. Angelika followed my lead, and together we leaned our bodies back until we touched the stairs and tilted our heads up towards the sky. BOOM went the fireworks, creating flowers that scattered across the sky. BOOM... BOOM! We passed the wine back and forth and laid there, talking about our jobs and plans for the future. I told her about my recent struggle with laundry day, something most foreigners dreaded, and laughed when I mentioned my still-wet shirt.

Angelika sat straight up with that.

"Anna! You cannot be outside with wet clothes on, you'll catch a chill!" She smiled at me, but her eyes were bewildered. "Come on, let's finish this bottle then get you someplace warm."

We spent the next fifteen minutes passing the bottle back and forth, watching as the group of fireworks lovers sent the last explosions flying into the air. We giggled as the soot rained down on us, brushing the black mess from our hair. We placed our now-empty wine bottle on top of one of the spent fireworks boxes, thinking at least the trash would all be in one neat pile. It's not like there were trash cans around, anyway. Then we made our way to the broken escalator that provided passageway to and from the apartment complex and laughed as we took giant strides all the way down. It took a lot of leg work to walk down the escalator, but I found that with a slight bounding motion, it was still quicker than taking the stairs.

Reaching the bottom, we found the street completely empty. No pedestrians, no bicycles or electric motorbikes, and certainly no taxis.

"We'll just have to walk until we find a cab," said Angelika.

"Where do you want to go?" I asked.

"Why, English Corner, of course! I know they're still open!" she exclaimed.

Most of the bars in Jinan stayed open during the Spring Festival. There's always a place for the wicked and lonely. English Corner was a hole-in-the-wall bar with watered down drinks and a stinking atmosphere, but it was often the first bar that expats ventured to. Lured in with the word "English" in the bar's name, foreigners and locals alike expected the bar to be a haven for the English-speaking community.

It was not. Rather, most seasoned foreigners avoided the place. Located on the basement level, the liquor always tasted off, the cocktails were watered down, and the bathrooms were always backed up. Yet, sometimes you just wanted a seedy place to rest in, and all the taxi drivers knew where this bar was. English Corner was always, always open it seemed, no matter what holiday or occasion. And even better, it was within walking distance to three other bars that lined Thousand Buddha Mountain Street.

We descended the steps to the bar and immediately heard a familiar laugh. It was Jozie! While most of the other French Canadians had opted for travel, Jozie had chosen to stay behind, saving up her money to put towards the flight to bring her wife to China. Jozie was pre-transition at this time, but her thick brown hair fell in waves past her shoulders, and the bartender was jesting about how "pretty of a girl" she was, despite looking like a man.

"Angelika!" Jozie exclaimed when she saw us, placing a hand gently on her shoulder. "It's so good to see you here! I thought everyone else was gone."

"Everyone else *is* gone," she laughed. "We're the only three left in the whole city!"

This wasn't true, of course, there were plenty of foreigners around, but we were scattered so thin that we felt rather alone. It was pure chance to end up at the same bar at the same time on the same night without any coordination.

"My *gomer* (bro) here is about to light off some firecrackers," she said, pointing to a balding man coming out of the bathroom, cigarette hanging from his lips. "Come outside and join us."

We ordered ourselves a round of beer. It was delivered warm. Then we followed Jozie's friend back up the stairs and out to the sidewalk. The balding man reached inside his jacket pocket and pulled out a strand of five firecrackers. But these were no average, little red firecrackers. Instead, they were enormous, at least four inches in length and as thick around as the neck of a wine bottle. Covered in white paper, they were like nothing I'd ever seen before.

"Oh, these are gonna hurt the ears," Jozie murmured, taking a sip of her beer.

Angelika backed up against the building's wall as the balding man hung the giant firecrackers from one of the small trees that lined the sidewalk.

"I don't think I want to actually hear this!" she said frantically. "Too loud! Too loud! Anna! Cover your ears!"

I stepped back a few paces and held my hands up over my ears as the balding man took his cigarette from his mouth and held it up to the surprisingly short fuse. When it sparked, he laughed, threw his cigarette down, and jumped backwards just before the firecrackers exploded with the loudest CRACK! CRACK! CRACK! CRACK! CRACK! I'd ever heard, before or since. I could feel my ears ringing when it was over. Jozie was hopping up and down with glee.

"That was the best!" she cried, as she patted her friend on

the back hard and handed him a new cigarette. He thanked Jozie and, smiling, returned back inside. We spent the rest of the night together at the bar before making our way home at sunrise, planning to get together several times over the next ten days. We never saw our firecracker friend again, but the memory of just how loud those firecrackers were still rings in our heads to this day.

Despite making the best of our new year's nights, being able to truly experience the Spring Festival like a local was something that I'd always coveted. Our Chinese friends were always more than happy to involve us in the other festivities throughout the year, bringing us to their apartments for meals and traveling with us for themed experiences. The new year was trickier though, since most individuals traveled out to the countryside and nobody wanted to burden their older relatives with the task of catering to a foreigner. Where would they sleep? Would there be enough to eat? How much time would having this person with me take away from spending time with my family?

But by the time the 2013 Spring Festival rolled around, I had a Chinese boyfriend. He gave himself the English name Alan, although he spoke very little English. We worked together at the same English training school in the LiXia district of Jinan. There, he was a marketing manager, in charge of public marketing events to pull students into the classrooms. But the job didn't pay much despite its importance, and when Alan and I first started dating, his apartment looked more like rubble after a wartime effort than someplace someone should live. As a result, I asked him to move in with me a mere month after we started dating. By this time I was working as an English teacher in Jinan and had my own two-bedroom apartment all to myself. We were head over heels in love with each other and, as a show of good faith, Alan asked me to join him in his hometown for the holiday.

Alan was from a tiny village in Inner Mongolia, about an hour's drive from the city of Chifeng. Chifeng was sparsely populated with less than four-million people, and was coated in a fine layer of white dust that rolled in off the grassless plains, or so I'd heard Alan say. Luckily, there was a long-distance bus that traveled directly from Jinan to Chifeng, stopping only once in Beijing. It was a 12-hour overnight journey, but it was cheaper and much less crowded than the train. Driving a car on the interstate, you could make the journey in about nine hours. But the buses were slow and cumbersome, and they often broke down on long journeys. Planning to spend a week in his village, we packed the biggest suitcases we could find, including my heavy-duty camping backpack. There would be no way to wash our clothes there, he warned, so we packed enough for the whole seven days.

Leaving at 6pm on a Wednesday afternoon we reached the city of Chifeng at noon the next day, hours after we were scheduled to arrive. The bus had stopped at a rest station every four hours to let us all eat and relieve ourselves. But each time, the driver had fallen asleep in a location other than the bus, and he had to be tracked down. The bus had also broken down twice before reaching Baoding, and furthermore, the delays put us right in the middle of Beijing morning traffic. Since everyone else was also trying to leave the city to make their way home, we were stuck bumper-to-bumper for hours.

But somehow, we reached Chifeng by lunch time. Alan and I stood outside the bus station, drawing lines in the sidewalk dust with our shoes. It would still be another hour's car ride before we reached his village, so we shared a cigarette before finding a cab driver willing to take us the distance. As we rode, I watched the sparse high-rise buildings turn into golden fields of broken stalks.

"It's sunflowers," Alan told me. "That's what they farm here."

"Is that what your parents farm, too?" I asked. I knew very little about Alan's parents except that they both lived in a tiny village and they had a good relationship with both of their sons.

"Well," he replied, "my village farms both sunflowers and poplar trees. And my dad works in the gold mine during the off-season."

I couldn't help but notice Alan wringing his hands. This was the first time he was bringing a girl home to his family, and casual dating wasn't really a "thing" in China. If you were dating, the end game was marriage. Despite my party nature, I wasn't one for casual relationships, and could easily see myself marrying Alan. So not only was Alan bringing a foreign home girl to his parents, but he was also taking a foreign girl whom he hoped to marry to his incredibly poor village. I knew he was concerned about the disparity between our separate families' finances (I grew up soldily middle-class), and I tried to reiterate to him that those things just didn't matter to me, but he was still quite nervous. I took his hand in mine and held it tightly. The taxi driver was delightfully silent.

We traveled down a maze of side roads before eventually stopping in front of a courtyard surrounded by a six-foot high mud-brick wall. A small iron gate opened in the middle of the wall, and beyond it lay Alan's house. There were maybe fifteen homes in the village, all built in the same style. The houses all had three rooms. Walking directly into the houses meant entering the kitchen first. On either side of the kitchen sat a two-and-a-half-foot high tile counter, and inside the counter was a massive cast iron wok, laid neatly inside the counter so that its iron brim met the tiles. The counters were hollow, and a wide hole sat at the front bottom of each counter for a fire to be built underneath and heat the wok.

The kitchen had two additional rooms built onto either side, and these rooms were also identical. Attached to the wall closest to the kitchen sat a *kang,* or a raised concrete bed about three feet off the ground. Each *kang* spanned the entirety of the front wall of the room, about ten feet, with two wide windows in front of the *kangs* to let in light. The underside of the *kang* was hollow, and attached by a small vent to underneath the kitchen fire area. To keep the beds warm at night, fires would be built in the kitchen and heat would travel through the vents and under the beds.

The floors were all concrete, and a black wood burning stove was placed in the center of each of the rooms, save the kitchen. Each room had a set of counters and shelves, and the kitchen had a nice glass cabinet. Some houses had more shelves and cabinets, sturdy wooden tables, and permanent seating aside from the *kangs,* which was where most entertaining took place. Alan's house was comparatively bare.

Walking through the gated entrance of the courtyard, I saw Alan's mother push the heavily padded cotton blanket hanging above the doorway open and eagerly step outside. She didn't run to hug him, nor did he hug her when we approached.

"You look so good, son," she said smiling, running her fingers across his sleeve. Most Chinese families do not show physical affection in the same way Westerners do. I-love-you's are exceedingly rare and hugging is reserved for young children. Alan even had a hard time adjusting to my insistence at getting a goodbye kiss every time he left the house. "Can't you just *see* that I love you?" he'd asked. We compromised with a kiss each morning before work. My foreign girl friends would scoff and say that I was giving in, but I didn't think it was fair for Alan to have to change while I didn't.

"Mom, this is Anna," he told his mother, gesturing my way.

I didn't think her smile could grow any larger, but she turned to me, grinning ear to ear, mouth open and eyes sparkling. She was slightly taller than Alan with flowing black hair that reached her mid-shoulders. She kept it in a ponytail under a yellow scarf tied around her head and under her chin. Her clothes were dirty, but not tattered. They just hadn't been washed in a while – it was customary to wear the same clothes for up to a week during the winter months.

"It's so good to meet you," I told her. "Thank you for welcoming me to your home."

"It's nothing," she said, "I'm just happy my oldest has finally brought a girl home for the new year. Come, let me get your things."

I protested as Alan's mother tried to pick up my large camping backpack. It was heavy. Still, she insisted, and I knew the polite thing would be to let her take it. So, I watched her carry it off into the house while Alan and I followed behind. She set my backpack on the *kang* in the right-hand side of the house.

"You'll sleep here tonight," she said, and pointed to a large pile of blankets neatly folded up in a corner. "We'll light a fire to make sure you're warm."

Just then, Alan's father came through the front door, dragging behind him a pile of straw. Not noticing we were there, he began stuffing the straw into the bottom hole of one of the kitchen stoves. Alan called out to him, and he jumped in surprise. A little taller and much dirtier than his wife, I could immediately tell where Alan got his good looks. His father's skin was almost as dark as Alan's, and both men looked a shade of red rather than being yellow. In China, people truly prided themselves on being the "yellow people", frequently calling themselves yellow in a manner that left most native English speakers baffled.

After patting his son on the back, Alan's father turned to me and held out a hand. I took it and shook it, appreciative of the gesture.

"Show her around before your brother gets here and you two get distracted," he told Alan. "I still have some work to do around the house." With that, he exited, walking out of the courtyard and turning towards the larger part of the village.

Leading me outside, Alan first took me behind the house. There, a mud-brick silo had been built, about seven feet high, with a large wooden door in the roof and another on the side. "This is like our refrigerator," he explained. I looked inside and saw an assortment of vegetables, grains, and other perishables. Back in the courtyard, he then showed me the storage shed. It was the size of one of the bedrooms in the house, and full of farming equipment. On the opposite side of the courtyard sat the chicken run, and behind that was the toilet.

"Be careful not to fall in," Alan told me as we stared at the hole in the ground with wooden planks over top to place your feet. "I doubt you could actually fall inside, but you might slip and lose a shoe." He spoke from experience.

"What do you do when it gets full?" I asked.

"Dad takes a shovel and gets inside," he said, pointing at the hole. "The village uses it as fertilizer."

I was lost in contemplation when I heard a loud bray. Turning quickly to the left, I saw Alan's father leading two mules through the courtyard. I lit up.

"Can I pet them? Oh please!" I begged, but Alan shook his head.

"No, they're mean. The only person they're nice to is my father," he said as we watched a mule kick at a chicken that had gotten a little too close to a back leg.

Alan laughed as I frowned. "I know you like animals. Come on, I'll take you to some mules you can pet!"

He grabbed my hand, leading me out of the courtyard and into the village proper. The roads were all dirt, with huge ruts carved out in the most well-traveled of places. Each of the houses looked almost identical, with the only difference being the types and colors of tiles that some houses had plastered on the outside in place of brick. These homes, built and paid for by the government, were the newer houses, but the layout and size were the same as the others. Chickens, goats, and dogs ran freely through the village. I tried to pet as many as possible, but even the dogs were shy. Finally, we came to a house with a large, old mule hitched to the front gate.

"You can pet him," Alan said, "He's old and sweet."

"Won't the neighbors get upset?" I asked.

"No," Alan laughed. "They'll just be happy to see me!"

After I'd had my fill of the old, sweet mule, Alan led me to a dilapidated house in the middle of the village.

"This is my house," he said. "It used to be my grandfather's, but he died. Since I'm the oldest son, I get to inherit it. But I want to fix it up before I bring my family here," he explained. I tried to picture myself living and raising children in the house, the thought of which struck me as overwhelmingly boring with not much to see or explore. I shook off the thought, though, reminding myself that this was the place that produced the man I loved and trying to remember that not everyone was born into luck like me. Besides, maybe I'd actually enjoy the seclusion if we married and lived here.

When we returned to Alan's family home, his mother was diligently lighting incense to place on a small brick shelf jutting out near the door. Above the shelf was a red and yellow picture of what looked like a deity.

"I thought you said your parents weren't religious?" I asked, exceedingly curious.

"They're not, not like Buddhists or anything. But they do worship our ancestors," Alan said.

We spent the remainder of the afternoon back inside the house, sitting on the *kang*. Fellow villagers came and went, eager to see Alan and his foreign girlfriend. The younger children wouldn't come past the doorway, except for a very brave five-year-old who demanded to hear me speak English. My hair, which at this point was still in dreadlocks that cascaded all the way down my back, especially enamored them. Alan's younger brother arrived a few hours later, and his mother busied herself in the kitchen while the men and I sat drinking tea and talking about life in the big city. Before dinner, we all helped pull out the fold-up table used as the dining room table, and collected the folding chairs scattered throughout the house.

His mother truly made a feast. Stir-fried green beans and strips of beef. Scrambled eggs and green onion sprouts. Pork dumplings. Vinegar cucumber salad. The dishes were simple, but abundant, and they tasted better than any restaurant I'd eaten at. The dumplings, especially, were like magic in my mouth. They had butchered their last hog to make the dumplings especially in my honor, and I had to hold myself back from eating them too greedily. Mid-way through dinner, I set down my chopsticks and gasped.

"I've forgotten something!" I said, and stood up from my seat. "Please excuse me." I began rummaging around my backpack until my fingers found something smooth and cold. I pulled out a bottle of Jim Beam and presented it to Alan's father.

"This is alcohol from near my hometown," I told him.

Alan's father grinned, stood up, and opened the closest cabinet door. Pulling out a large, clear bottle, he said, "This is alcohol I made right here! I'll try yours if you try mine!"

I agreed, and his father poured the homemade moonshine into five little glasses, handing one out to each of us. "*Ganbei!*" he shouted, then threw the contents of the glass back in his throat. We all followed suit. (*Ganbei* means "dry glass", meaning drink the whole shot.) It felt like fire hit my throat and I gasped for air. That was the strongest alcohol I'd ever tasted! Alan's father laughed.

"Very good, very good," he said approvingly. "Now let's try yours."

Pouring a round of whiskey, we all *ganbei'd* again. Alan's mother gave a sound of delight, and his father made an "ahh" sound that ended in a grin.

"It's good! It's good!" he bellowed. "Tomorrow, I'll share with the rest of the family!"

We went to bed early that night, almost as soon as it had gotten dark. Alan and I slept on one *kang* while his mother, brother, and father slept in the other room. Despite the deep cold, Alan and I were still able to find some comfort in each other.

The next day for breakfast, I watched Alan's mom pull last night's leftovers out of a cupboard and reheat them in the giant wok. The kitchen stayed cold enough at nights to preserve a bit of food. The dumplings tasted just as good for breakfast as they did for dinner.

By 10:00am, the house was full of people again. Alan's mother's family – two sisters, a brother, their respective spouses, and her mother – had all come to visit for the Spring Festival, and to see Alan and his brother for the first time in a year, and of course, to meet me. Their clothes were dusty, but mine were getting the same way after less than 24 hours in the village. They were loud, and full of laughter. They all sat in a circle on the *kang*, eating sunflower seeds and drinking hot green tea. I sat on the outskirts of the circle, leaning against the wall, and took it all in. I tried to follow the conversation, but had a hard time with the dialect, and they were speaking about family drama. At lunchtime, Alan and I set up the folding table and found enough chairs to seat everyone. True to his word, Alan's father broke out the Jim Beam and began portioning it out to the guests.

"Do you like to drink alcohol?" Alan's grandmother leaned in to ask me as lunch was being served.

I flushed. "I do," I admitted, "I drink a lot of it, actually." I was worried this would make me a "bad girl" in their eyes, as most women in China neither smoked nor drank.

"I do, too," she giggled, then picked up her glass to toast me. She downed the whiskey without a grimace. I followed suit.

"Be careful," Alan's father said, shaking his chopsticks at me. "She'll drink you under the table!"

"I can accept that challenge," I said, smirking, and Alan's aunts clapped.

"Last person at the table wins, then," one of the aunts said, and poured the last dregs of whiskey into our glasses.

"Don't worry, I brought more baijiu," said Alan's uncle. I groaned inside. Baijiu was not only strong, but tasted like death. Made out of sorghum, its distinct smell could singe the hair right out of your nose, but that doesn't deter the Chinese. Alan's mother stood up from the table. "I don't want to get drunk right now, so I'll just watch," she said.

"I can't play this game, either," Alan said. "I lose every time." And with that, Alan and his brother left the table. They encouraged me to stay, however, so I did.

We sat and talked, and ate, and drank, and drank some more. About every fifteen minutes, an aunt or uncle would call out "*ganbei!*" and we would drain our glasses. After three drinks, Alan's father left the table.

"I need a cigarette," he mumbled as he reached for his pack in his back pocket and sat on the *kang*.

"Why get up when you can just have one at the table?" Alan's grandma chuckled, and pulled out her own pack of cigarettes. As she handed me one, I decided that I liked his family. His own grandma smoked and drank, meaning she was a "bad girl" like me. They invited me, a stranger, into their drinking game. And they weren't asking prying questions like, "when will you have children?"

"*Ganbei!*" Alan's grandma called, and we all downed our drinks. Alan's uncle stood up this time, and as he made his way to the *kang* to sit with his brother-in-law, we could hear Alan's father softly snoring.

Our bellies were sufficiently full, but the food remained on the table so we could pick at a bite here and there between the conversation and drinking. I handed Alan's grandma a cigarette from my pack, and she took it smiling. It's customary to share cigarettes in China.

This time, an aunt called out, "*ganbei!*" But after draining my glass, I felt a little queasy. The feeling grew, and as I burped, I knew I couldn't continue anymore. I stood up from the table.

"You beat me, for sure!" I exclaimed. "You're a strong one!"

Alan's grandma chuckled. "I beat everybody," she said, and called for another drink.

I returned to my previous seat on the *kang*, back against the wall, sitting cross-legged and feeling delightfully dizzy. Alan's mother came into the room and reached over me to grab a thick, green blanket. She gingerly draped it over the front of me, tucking the blanket behind my shoulders and patting my head.

"You sleep now," she said, laughing quietly.

In front of me, Alan's father and uncle were both snoring, both drunk and needing the rest. Alan and his brother were still outside. Alan's mother took a seat at the table, but refused a drink. As the two aunts and grandmother kept drinking, I let myself slip off to sleep. A mid-day nap sounded perfect.

After the nap, the rest of the day passed much the same as the day before. It seemed like the only things to do were sit, talk, and eat sunflower seeds. Later, Alan and his brother took me through the fields of poplar trees up to the gold mine that sat about a half-mile away from the village. There wasn't much to see except for a gated entrance, but we played on the physical recreation equipment for some time before heading back. When we arrived back at Alan's house, his mother stood outside scraping scraps of noodles into a small metal bowl. Suddenly, three cats came bounding out from around the courtyard and huddled around the bowl, hungrily chomping at the noodles.

On the evening of the New Year, we gathered around the small tv in the right-hand room and watched the Chinese Spring Festival Gala. An annual event, the gala is full of comedy routines, skits, classic operas, and amazingly talented people from across the country. When Alan's mom made dumplings this time, she put a little coin in three of the dumplings. Whoever got the coins was said to have good luck in the next year. I got one. Alan's brother got two. At the stroke of midnight, we all went outside and lit off fireworks. The rest of the village did the same, and soon a haze of smoke and light surrounded us. We all went to bed immediately after the fireworks were over. After that, the partying was over.

When I woke up the next day, my eyes were terribly itchy. I couldn't keep my hands from rubbing them, and giant tears welled up in my eyes with each touch. I thought it was just allergies and tried to go along with my day, following Alan around the village and talking with the local people, but soon, my vision started to become blurry. My eyes started to burn an hour later, and it was a struggle to keep them open. The only relief I felt was when my eyes were closed, and even then, they itched something fierce. I asked to see a doctor.

"There's a bus that can take us into Chifeng, but we have to walk to meet it, and if you want to go, we'd better hurry. It leaves in an hour," Alan said.

"How far of a walk is it?" I asked.

"About thirty minutes, but with the snow…" he trailed off.

The snow had fallen a good eleven inches since we'd gotten into town. This generally wasn't a problem in terms of transportation or simply walking around, but getting to the bus would mean walking through the fields, which meant trudging through the snow unless we wanted to take the long way.

I let out a deep sigh. I wanted to cry, but crying wouldn't get me any closer to the hospital. With temperatures well below freezing, I layered up my warmest clothes and wrapped myself in a scarf. Alan helped me put my hat, gloves, and heavy boots on before bundling himself in his warm winter coat. He then took my hand, and began leading me out of his house and into the snow-laden fields. It was a long, hard trudge across the terrain, and at times the wind would blow so cold against my face, I couldn't help but close my eyes as I walked, gripping Alan's hand.

"We have to be quicker if we want to catch the bus," Alan urged.

I let out a whimper, but quickened my pace. My eyes burned, they were leaking fluid, and by now my vision was just a blur. Still, I knew I couldn't miss the bus if I wanted any chance of relief, so I clenched my teeth tightly and forced my legs to take bigger, faster strides.

We reached the bus stop with ten minutes to spare before its scheduled arrival. We smoked while we waited, my eyes closed the whole time. The bus ran late due to the weather, but once it stopped, Alan paid the fare for both of us and helped me to a seat in the back. It would be an hour-and-a-half's ride into the city.

"I hate when everybody stares," Alan whispered, clearly annoyed.

"You'll get used to it," I told him. "I'm used to it by now." But Alan was still new to getting stared at, all brought about by his relationship with a foreigner. When we were together, he received quite a bit of attention. He didn't like it.

By the time we arrived in Chifeng, my vision was completely blurred over, no matter how much I rubbed or blinked my eyes. We didn't go to the main hospital, but rather a small clinic. The doctor saw me directly in her office. She gingerly touched around my face and eyes, asked me questions about my facial hygiene routine for the past few days, and investigated my eyesight with a set of flashlights.

"It's keratitis," the doctor said. "You probably got it from washing your face with the water in your village. Did you boil it before you washed with it?"

"No," I admitted, "I just used the same water everyone else was."

"Well unboiled water is still full of viruses and bacteria,

and sometimes parasites," she explained, "but some antibiotics should clear it right up."

She wrote down the information and handed it to Alan, who navigated to the pharmacy. I was given three days' worth of amoxicillin with three 100mg pills per day. Not enough to be an effective dose, but it was all I had. I tore the first pill from the package while standing on the sidewalk, swallowing it down dry.

The pills helped, but the itching never really went away. Six months later, I would return to the US to visit my family, and decided to schedule an appointment with an ophthalmologist. The doctor told me that it was the worst case of keratitis that he'd ever seen, told me that it was worse than textbook images, and called in the other two practicing eye doctors to have a look, too. I was told I was lucky to have never gone blind.

Evening had already fallen by the time we returned to Alan's tiny village. His mother apologized profusely for not having hot water to wash our faces with, but I tried my best to make sure she knew this wasn't her fault and that it could happen to anyone. She boiled our washing water for the rest of the week's stay. When we left for Jinan on Friday, she sent us home with two giant bags of dumplings since we had a freezer to store them in. She was delighted that I'd liked them so much that she'd made extras. The trip home took significantly less time.

Alan and I were still together for the next year's Spring Festival, and so we once again traveled to his home village together. This time, however, we would make a side journey to see his grandmother, who lived in a larger village of fifty houses about three hours north of Chifeng. I remember trying to explore the hills around the village with Alan's cousins, but the frozen wind of Inner Mongolia was so biting that it made the metal piercing in my ear burn with threatened frostbite. Alan's fingers were so cold, he could scarcely make a fist without pain. We didn't stay out long.

Later that afternoon, Alan's grandmother presented us with special thick slices of white cheese made from yak's milk and bowls of salty milk tea. Alan and his cousins sat eagerly around the sitting room table, dipping their cheese in the hot salty milk and thoroughly enjoying the snack. The cheese was too sour for me, however, and I couldn't accustom myself to the salty milk tea. Before Alan and I went to sleep that night, I saw his grandmother shove a fifty-yuan bill in his pocket.

"Grandma, no, that's too much!" Alan tried to protest, but it seems that grandmothers all over the world are fond of insisting their grandchildren take a little *extra* cash.

I was single for the next two Spring Festivals – Alan and I simply had different timelines for our lives – and decided to spend my days off in Jinan rather than attempt to travel abroad with many of the other foreign teachers. However, those of us who didn't travel banded together over the two-week period to stave off loneliness and enjoy the eerie silence of the city. At times, we would lay down in the red-paper-littered streets, waving our arms and legs to make angels in the waste. Some years, we would simply bar hop between the open establishments where the bar owners had become like second family. No matter the year, it always went out with a bang.

So You Think You're a Teacher?

As my first semester at the University of Shandong drew to a close, I knew I wanted to stay in China, but my grades were nowhere near good enough for my American university to approve of my re-enrollment through their exchange program. If I wanted to attend classes again in the fall, I'd be all on my own. That meant tuition, room and board, and basic living expenses would have to be covered by yours truly, and as a blossoming nineteen-year-old, I thought to myself, "surely, *something* is bound to work out...right?" And in fact, it didn't take long before a friend of a friend gave my name and number to a university employee from the other side of campus who had connections with an English program at a high school in a neighboring city.

In order to teach English in China legally, you needed at least a bachelor's degree, and schools had a strong preference for native English speakers with TEFL certificates. I had no prior teaching experience and no degree, or any form of certification for that matter, but the facts that I was white, female, and a native-English speaker *from America* were all that mattered to Mr. Liu. Native English speakers who didn't already have jobs were hard to come by in the city. Most were locked into 2-year contracts with the handful of training schools in the area, although teachers could also be found scattered about in high schools and universities, depending on their experience and willingness to work long hours. Still, a good number of non-native speakers and speakers from other English-speaking countries aside from the US were able to find part-time jobs at the smaller and possibly unlicensed training schools without issue. All money was delivered under the table, so if the school or the teacher were caught, everyone could claim it was a volunteer program. Then the school would grease the palms of whatever officer was officially (or unofficially, in many cases) investigating, and all would be forgotten.

I'd made money like this on a few occasions too. Friends would ask me to substitute for them while sick or on vacation. However, the job was always messy – I was never given any instruction on *how* to teach, and sometimes given no information on *what* to teach, either. But with a going rate of 100 yuan per hour, the money was easy and fast. Mr. Liu's deal for me beat anything my fellow university students had been offered: teach American Culture and History as a summer program at Tai'an Number 2 High School from 8:00am to 12:00pm, Monday through Friday, for 10,000 yuan (1,500 USD) per month. Housing was also provided. 10,000 yuan a month was an absurd amount of money, much more than the average monthly training school salary of around 7,000 yuan. My rent was a mere 1,200 yuan a month. Once I heard that figure, I knew I would be taking the job.

The city of Tai'an was approximately an hour away by slow train. Rumor had it that the high-speed train being built would get you there in 20 minutes, but that project was still years away from completion. Tai'an was famous for Mount Tai, the highest point in Shandong province with an elevation of over 5,000 ft. While Tai'an technically encompassed large districts of farmland, home to 5 million people over 3,000 square miles, the metro area only housed 1.7 million people. Compared to Jinan's 7 million, the city felt like a small town. Boasting 3,000 years of culture due to the mountain's long-standing spiritual significance, Tai'an felt like something out of a 90's cartoon that stereotyped China as nothing but temples and firecrackers and street vendors and mystical, foggy scenery. I had visited before to climb the mountain, and had loved every moment of the adventure. So sure, I could live in Tai'an for the summer. "I'll just come home to Jinan on the weekends," I told myself.

Mr. Liu was delighted that I'd agreed to teach for the school, and once the weekend came, he picked me up in his black BMW to drive me to Tai'an and get a feel for what I'd be doing. My Chinese was much better than his English. As we started to drive, Mr. Liu handed me a small red and gray Nokia cell phone. It was as basic as cell phones could get, with no flipping or sliding actions and a black and white screen.

"This is your Tai'an cell phone," he told me. "It's got a SIM card from the city in it, so you won't have to worry about extra charges."

I looked the phone over and thanked him for the gift. I'd heard talk from my European friends that Nokia's were essentially indestructible, but this was my first time with the brand. The display screen was all of 1.5 inches with alphanumeric keys and two arrows for scrolling. It couldn't take pictures, but it did come with both snake and sudoku games. I pried off the back to take a look inside and found two SIM card slots. I never had to worry about SIM cards before coming to China, but I knew that having two slots was a big deal.

"I added myself to your contact list already, and I'll send you a text with your number when we get to Tai'an," said Mr. Liu.

Then a wide smile swept across his face. "This is my favorite song!" he exclaimed, reaching to turn up the volume of the radio. He began to sing, "*mei na me jian dan...*" and belted out the entire song unabashedly. People weren't embarrassed about singing in China. It didn't matter if you sounded good or not, everybody loved to sing, and karaoke was a popular pastime. Walking through the city, it was common to pass plenty of people singing to themselves on the streets. I still wasn't quite used to it and felt surprised every time it happened. In America, you're weird if you sing in public or in social situations, and people assume you're trying to show off. Mr. Liu continued singing for the next hour.

When we arrived in Tai'an, Mr. Liu told me he wanted me to join him for lunch at his favorite restaurant just outside the city. It served only local cuisine. I agreed, of course, happy to fill my belly and knowing that it would be rude to refuse. We drove up a steep gravel road towards a restaurant shaped like a pagoda with large traditional characters above the entryway, although I couldn't read what they said. The hostess seemed to know Mr. Liu, making conversation with him as she led us to a table outside under a pavilion. Vines swirled up the pavilion's thick wooden beams, rustling in the wind.

"Look!" cried out Mr. Liu, pointing at the vines. "A gecko!"

Sure enough, a small, grey gecko was scuttling up one of the beams, weaving in and out of the vines.

"They're all over the place here," said Mr. Liu. "It's like a symbol of the city. I even have one on my car! People keep them in their houses to eat the bugs, too."

I reached for my phone to take a picture, only to remember that the Nokia had no camera. By the time I'd grabbed my American phone, the gecko was gone.

"Don't worry," Mr. Liu reassured me, "there'll be plenty more."

He ordered three dishes and six bottles of Qingdao beer served warm. The beer was low enough in alcohol content that even three of the twenty-one-ounce bottles would get neither of us drunk, or even tipsy, especially while eating, but the beer always made me feel full. While refreshing even when warm, I knew it would be an effort to both eat and drink enough to be polite. The dishes arrived one by one. First was a thin, sour pancake made of fermented corn. It was soft on the tongue, yet slightly rubbery on the teeth. Next came what appeared to be a sweetened turnip cake made with red bean paste. Pan-seared on either side, the cake had a crisp but heavy texture. Last came Mr. Liu's favorite dish – deep fried grub worms.

Each grub was as long as a finger and twice as thick, beady eyes poking out on top of their crispy, golden bodies. I'd never eaten bugs before, and sitting there with a plate of them in front of me, I felt my stomach begin to turn. Mr. Liu picked up two with his chopsticks and set them on my plate, the biggest smile on his face. I knew I couldn't refuse him now. I fumbled with my chopsticks as I grabbed at one of the grubs, biting off the bottom half. It tasted just like a French fry. The guts inside were, thankfully, neither gushing nor gooey, but rather resembled the texture of mashed potatoes. I didn't hate it. In fact, I enjoyed the taste, and the two of us ate every last grub.

We took no leftovers with us. Not because we didn't have any, but because it was considered a sign of stinginess and poverty to take your food away from the table, and Mr. Liu was not a man who wanted to lose face.

"We'll go to your apartment next," he said, opening the car door for me before embarking on the twenty-minute drive to the apartment complex, located just southeast of Mount Tai. As we drove past the mansion of a hotel at the entrance of the complex, we could see the heavy construction of three-story single homes for the nouveau riche surrounding a small lake to the north, and a huge plaza of apartments and shops standing as unoccupied concrete cutouts to the south. My apartment was across the street from a flashy KTV, located on the 5th floor above a small hotel. The hotel only took up three stories, the other seven floors all occupied as loft apartments.

The apartment was small, just large enough for a queen size bed, two nightstands, and a dresser. The moderately-sized bathroom was complete with a western toilet, for which I was grateful, and the solarium doubled as a kitchen. Mr. Liu was proud to show me the blankets and cookware he'd bought me, though I'd be on my own for sheets and utensils. The apartment was paid for not by the school, but by Mr. Liu himself. At the time, I didn't find this odd. Most schools had foreign teacher managers that, well, managed all aspects of the foreigners, including apartments. We stayed long enough to tour the apartment – just a few minutes – before heading to the high school approximately two miles away, a distance that I would later find to be enjoyably walkable.

A high stone wall with rod iron spikes encircled the school grounds, deterring anyone who might try to climb over. Getting inside the school grounds meant speaking to the front guard, who retracted an electric metal gate and allowed Mr. Liu's car to pass through. He parked in the middle of the grounds, with no care that he might be obstructing somebody's way, then led me to my new classroom. Located on the first floor, the classroom had enough seats for 60 students, although I would only be teaching five. The desks and chairs were all wooden and vintage, and at the front of the room sat a plain podium in front of a large, dusty chalkboard. Giant windows lined the concrete walls on either side of the classroom, letting light filter from outside the building all the way into the hallways.

"This room is the only one with a projector," Mr. Liu said pointing first to the ceiling where the projector sat, then to the rolled-up projector screen above the chalkboard. "You have a computer, right? I'll give you the cables to hook everything up," he said.

"I do have a laptop," I said nodding, then asked, "When will I get the materials to teach?"

"Oh, you'll have to come up with that on your own," he said. "The course's topic is American culture and history. You want to get your students ready for life in America, since they all plan on going to American universities. So, you'll know what to teach them better than us."

We lingered in the classroom for a moment as I looked around, tracing a line in the dust of the concrete floor with my shoe. "So, does it all look good to you?" asked Mr. Liu.

"Yes, it all seems wonderful," I said with a smile, although inside I was feeling unsure if I was really up to the task of pulling this curriculum out of my ass.

"Great!" Mr. Liu exclaimed. "You'll start on Monday."

And so began my teaching career. I had absolutely no clue what I was doing, but I was great at faking it. I would spend Saturday working on presentations for the upcoming week, everything from what foods to expect (like hunks of meat and casseroles) to what manners were expected (like queuing in a straight line and not spitting on the ground), and history lessons from colonization (what *really* happened with the natives) to modern times (time to learn some economics). On Sunday nights, I would ride the next-to-last train into Tai'an, returning to Jinan via the same train on Friday nights. I found much joy in these train rides.

I would always purchase a hard seat ticket, but spent most

of my time milling about at the ends of the train cars, where the doors sat open as smokers filed in and out of the makeshift smoking section. I was smoking half a pack a day by now, and lighting up was certainly one way to kill time. The ends of the train cars were also prime real estate for those with standing-only tickets. Most of these ticket holders were migrant workers or construction crews, all men traveling between working in one city and living in another, thankful that their train ride home was less than an hour's commute. They always tried to speak to me, and I always tried to respond to them. Neither of us could understand much of what the other was saying, but they would laugh at my grammar mistakes and gently correct me in ways much more efficient than any classroom I'd been in. They taught me street slang, idioms, ways to address friends, and how to express affection for your peers without sounding so formal and rigid. They taught me how to speak like a local, and I soaked up as much as they were offering, sharing cigarettes the whole way.

In Tai'an, my five students ranged in age from fifteen to nineteen years old. The nineteen-year-old was a young woman who had already completed her first year of university and had come back to her old high school just to complete this program. She was scheduled to attend an American university in the fall. She was slightly shocked to learn that I was only a few months older than her, but said she didn't mind because I could provide her insight into what people her age would be like. One day during a break I caught three of my students down the hall in an unlocked classroom with all the windows open. They were smoking. They looked at me with wide eyes as I entered the room and quickly hid their cigarettes behind their backs.

I chuckled. "It's okay, I want to smoke, too," I said, "and there's no place to smoke outside. Just throw the butts away when you're done, and I won't tell anybody." Then I lit up my own cigarette and joined their circle. These cigarettes became a ritual during breaks. All six of us would steal away into the unlocked classroom. The fifteen-year-old girl, seventeen-year-old boy, and nineteen-year-old girl all smoked with me while the two other sixteen-year-old boys sat and watched. I knew I couldn't stop them from smoking. Everybody smoked in China – it was almost a hobby. But at least this way, I could get to know them more. During our breaks, we spoke Chinese, something we weren't allowed to do in the classroom. They told me of their hopes and dreams for the future, of the complications they had with their boyfriends and girlfriends, how their parents treated them, and what it was like living in the school's dormitories away from home during the week.

Connecting with them in this way made them all better students. Where they were sluggish in response before, now they raised their hands eagerly to answer my questions. Their essays transformed from short, dull reiterations to longer and more expressive works. They memorized names and dates and culture points, all showed up to class early, and I heard them practicing their English together before and after class. All of them passed my course.

At the end of the summer, Mr. Liu approached me with an offer. He told me that all of the students gave me so much praise that the school wanted to retain me as an official teacher. This time, they wanted me to teach the SAT to a group of 45 students, meeting every Monday, Wednesday, and Friday between the hours of 10:00am to 12:00pm and again from 1:00pm to 2:00pm. I would keep the same salary and the same apartment in Tai'an, and once my student visa expired, the school would give me a new work visa. At that point, I had a big decision to make

– I could either continue making bank as a teacher and save up my money, putting university on hold until I'd saved up enough to cover a year's worth of expenses, or head back to university knowing I'd need to find another job mid-semester to keep up with the cost food and housing. After a few days of deliberation, I decided to accept Mr. Liu's offer. I asked him how the school would be able to offer me a work visa considering I didn't have a degree, and he responded with, "don't worry about it." I'd heard plenty of stories of training schools creating fake diplomas for their teachers and paying the authorities to look the other way. So, I shrugged off any worries I had and decided to trust Mr. Liu.

The next day, Mr. Liu introduced me to the head of the international studies department from the high school, Mr. Xi. I was hoping Mr. Xi's English might be better than Mr. Liu's, but he spoke no English at all, and I found his accent difficult to understand. Mr. Liu informed me that we would be visiting a textbook warehouse that day to review possible texts for the upcoming semester. Thankfully, I had no immediate plans and could join them with ease. I didn't want to let my employer down by refusing him. We loaded up into Mr. Liu's BMW and drove to the outskirts of Jinan to the warehouse. The building was considerably smaller than the other surrounding warehouses, but the "new book smell" that emanated from its open bay doors was familiar and delightful. I followed behind Mr. Liu and Mr. Xi as a worker dressed in slacks and a tucked in polo shirt escorted us through the warehouse, stopping at all the English textbooks.

The issue, however, was that all of the textbooks were in Chinese, and none of them related to the SAT. Rather, most of the books were grammar and vocabulary books aimed at university students, but none of them were quite right. Mr. Liu and Mr. Xi expressed great disappointment when I told them this.

"*Nothing* here will work?" Mr. Liu asked.

"I mean, I could probably find a way to teach English using these books, but I can't read all the characters and it won't help the students prepare for the SAT," I replied.

"So, what do we need, then?" Mr. Xi inquired.

"In America, we studied using specific textbooks just for the SAT," I explained, "and I think the only way I can teach in a meaningful way is with those."

Mr. Liu thumbed through his phone. "Oh my God," he said, "they're so expensive."

"We'll see what we can do to get them," said Mr. Xi, placing a hand on my shoulder.

As we left the warehouse, I felt doubtful about what teaching materials I would end up with, worried that I would be left to make my curriculum completely on my own. I knew I would need to do a bit of restructuring depending on the general level of English ability in the classroom, but my only qualification for teaching the SAT was the fact that I'd done well on the SAT three years ago. However, a week before the official start of classes, Mr. Liu sent me a text on my Tai'an phone.

"I got the SAT books," he wrote. "They will be in the classroom when you start."

Sure enough, as I walked into the second-floor classroom on the first day of school, fifty SAT prep books sat on the teacher's desk in the front of the classroom, three years outdated. That was alright though, they could still get the job done. The students filed in at 9:50am and silently took their seats. Mr. Xi had provided me with a list of names for roll call. As I called out each student's name, I handed them a book and asked if they had an English name. Most of them did. The ones that didn't, wanted me to think of one for them. I gave them names like Victoria,

Liam, Judy, and Tyler. I asked everyone about their favorite food, color, and hobby, just to gauge their speaking ability. Some in the classroom spoke almost fluently. Others could barely understand what I was asking. Some students were merely freshmen while others were seniors, but their comprehension and vocabulary didn't seem to correspond to their individual grade levels. Teaching across such a wide variety of grades and abilities suddenly seemed very daunting, but I had no time to reconsider now. We had work to do.

The structure of the class focused on the grammar and vocabulary sections, putting a heavy emphasis on the multiple-choice questions. In the afternoons, we would switch to math. Their math skills far succeeded my own, and they all found even the hardest questions to be relatively easy. To hide my own mathematical deficits, I would write the problems out on the chalkboard and call on individual students to solve each step of the equation. I would ask, "do you think this is right?" at the end of each step. If the class responded positively, I would praise them then call on the next student to complete the next step. If the class responded negatively, I would ask for a volunteer to come up and fix the error. More often than not, I didn't know the correct steps or answers myself, but Mr. Xi praised my style of student-led learning, calling it innovative.

In China, students learn through rote memorization, and I quickly encountered a problem when it came to essay writing. Creative writing isn't taught until university, and isn't required for every degree, so some students go their entire educational career without it. In contrast, the SAT writing section aimed to analyze the students' writing skills based on a prompt, something that my students just couldn't handle.

"What's the right answer?" they would ask me. Their minds

exploded when I told them, "There is no right answer." To flex this particular brain muscle, I began assigning weekly writing prompts. I provided the beginning and end of a story, and they would be left to fill in the middle. Or I would create a prompt that required them to fill in their own nouns and adjectives, as a sort of mad-libs bastardization. Many of them copied off of another classmate... a particular group of six students always had the same stories written. But slowly, my students began getting better at filling in the missing pieces with their own creative narratives, although many expressed discomfort with the assignments, saying they were too hard.

One day, I was running about five minutes late, and my students were up and mingling around the classroom. The door to the classroom was closed, but thin enough that I could hear their conversation. They were flinging English curse words at each other, showing off all they had learned, except they were using these curses in the wrong contexts.

"I don't give an ass what you say!"

"Shit your mother!"

And my personal favorite, "Your shirt is so fuck!"

They all went pale when they saw me at the door. "We're sorry, Teacher Anna!" they exclaimed, and rushed back to their seats. I walked to the front of the classroom and stood behind the desk, surveying the room. You could hear a pin drop.

"Listen," I began, "everybody curses. Every language has its own curses, and I can tell you from experience that when you live in a new country, some of the first words you'll pick up and memorize are going to be curse words. That's just how our brains are wired."

"So here's what we're going to do," I continued, "we're going to take a vote on what we learn today. Either we can spend the first two hours of class learning about English curse words and how to use them the RIGHT way... because none of you were using them the right way... or we can continue on with our lessons as planned."

They stared at me, slightly stunned and blinking.

"I want everyone to close their eyes so we can take a vote," I said, "and if everyone votes 'yes', then we'll learn about curse words. But if just one person votes 'no', then we'll do the normal lesson. I don't want anybody to feel uncomfortable. So everyone, close your eyes." They all closed their eyes.

"If you would like to learn about English curse words, please raise your hand." Every hand in the classroom flew up immediately.

"Okay," I said. "Now if you would like to continue with our normal lesson, please raise your hand." The whole classroom was still, as if they were afraid that the slightest movement of their hands would be interpreted as a vote.

"Open your eyes," I said. They opened their eyes. "Today, we will learn about curse words!"

Before we began, I cautioned them that the school would probably get mad at me if they knew what I was teaching them that day, and while I personally felt it was important to use this opportunity to teach them proper context and grammar, very few would agree with me. Still, they were old enough to be using curse words in their daily language. I had heard plenty of Chinese curses as I walked the halls of the high school. And at least on this day, I had the attention of every single student.

To begin, I walked them through the use of shit, damn, hell, fuck, bastard, dick, and pussy, with the latter causing quite a stir. In Mandarin, the curse word "*niu bi*" translates to "cow pussy", and is used to say that something is absolutely amazing. I explained that in the English language, calling someone a pussy meant calling them a coward, and to really pay attention to the context and use of this word, because if you called a stranger on the street a "pussy" in America, you were likely to get punched instead of praised. They all scribbled in their notebooks with a ferocity I'd never seen before.

At the end of the lesson, I told the class that we couldn't ignore the writing for the day. Over the upcoming weekend, their homework assignment would be to write a short story about a knight and a dragon. This would be a bit of a challenge since stories about western knights weren't very popular in China. Furthermore, their story needed to have at least three paragraphs, and each paragraph needed at least four sentences. They could collaborate on ideas for characters, settings, and actions, but ultimately their stories needed to be their own. I wrote an example introduction on the board, knowing that most would copy word for word, but if I could get at least two paragraphs of original work from them, then the assignment would be a success.

Then a student raised his hand. "Can we write curse words in our story?" he asked with hope in his eyes.

I considered his request for a moment, and replied, "You may use ONE curse word, but it MUST be in the correct context or else I'll mark the sentence as incorrect." Smiles swept across the classroom as I dismissed my students for their lunch break.

"If there's one thing I can accomplish with this job," I thought to myself, "it's teaching people not to cuss like idiots."

At the end of next Monday's class, I asked my students to turn in their stories. I was delighted to see that every single student had a story to submit, and couldn't wait to start reading. What tales did these young people spin when they put pen to paper? Would their knights be brave? Would they survive the dragon? Would townsfolk get eaten? I sat down to dinner that night with my red pen, ready to grade.

There was a city with a castle. The knight lived in the castle. A dragon lived in a cave nearby. It was a big pussy dragon. Incorrect use of "pussy". Circle it in red.

Once upon a time, there was a big black pussy dragon. Circle it in red with "wrong context" written above.

A princess was captured by a dragon. He was very pussy. Oh, for heaven's sake! No! Wrong. Use. Of. Pussy.

My eyes scanned through the remaining papers. Every single one of my students had written about a pussy dragon, all using "pussy" in the wrong context. Paper after paper, the words pussy dragon repeated over and over, which was the most important curse word to watch out for! I thought we went over this? Didn't I see them all scribbling down every word that came out of my mouth? Slight infuriation rose up inside of me, but at the same time couldn't help roaring with laughter at every pussy dragon story I read. Occasionally, the knight would be very pussy, too. These were the kinds of papers I kept for my own pleasure, but I considered the assignment to be a wash. The class could try again next week, with a little more guidance from me and no more cursing from them. When I told them that they'd all used their chosen curse word incorrectly, they were shocked and saddened that I wouldn't reteach the cursing lesson. There was no time to go back, I told them, and if they wanted to learn how to curse better, they'd have to research it on their own. Sometimes, I'd pull these stories out at the parties I'd host in my apartment for other teachers to examine. The readers were always amused, some laughing until they cried.

As the school year progressed, so did my students. Their

grammar and vocabulary improved greatly, and about half of the students were able to write creatively with no prompts. Their paragraphs were short, but at least they were coming up with their own ideas. To get more students involved in a creative frame of mind, I would assign group projects that required each student to contribute a creative element. One such assignment was to create an advertisement for something you want to sell. They could choose to sell anything. The group with the darkest skinned student decided to sell him as chocolate, drawing up a billboard of his face with a bite taken out of it. Inadvertent racism was more common than expected. But as my students found themselves happier and happier in my classroom, I was becoming more and more anxious. My visa was set to expire in a few weeks, and I hadn't received my month's salary.

When I asked Mr. Liu about the situation, he told me that while the school was willing to sponsor my work visa, they weren't willing to pay for the expenses it took to get me that visa, and that my salary was being used to cover the visa costs. "You'll get the rest of what's left after we get you the visa," he tried to reassure me.

"But I need money *now*," I tried to explain. "I can barely feed myself!"

"I can bring you food," he said, "and your apartment is paid for by me, so you don't have to worry about rent."

"But I *do* have to worry about rent, Mr. Liu," I pushed. "I rented an apartment in Jinan after I left the university. That's where all of my belongings are. And that's where I stay on the weekends and during breaks. I have to pay my landlord! I don't want to stay in Tai'an all the time, all my friends are in Jinan."

He simply responded with an "oh", and was silent for a moment, thinking of what he should say next. He reassured me that everything would get sorted out in time and sent 1,000 yuan to my bank account to cover my daily living expenses in the meantime.

Two days later, I received a call from Mr. Liu. "I have a way to get your visa extended for now, just so you don't have to leave the country before you get your work visa," he said, "but you'll have to agree to do some things exactly the way I tell you." I listened as Mr. Liu explained that he had a friend who had a friend at the police station, an officer who would be willing to extend my visa in exchange for a bribe. This was common enough, and all we had to do was put on a good show, perform the right song and dance, and nobody would bat an eye.

"You'll have to pretend like you broke your leg and couldn't get on a plane home," explained Mr. Liu, "so you'll have to look like your leg still hurts. But I'll do all the talking. After class on Friday, we'll go down to the Security Bureau. Just follow my lead. Oh, and it will be costly, so you won't be able to get your salary again. But I'll give you a little walking around money, okay?"

What else could I do but agree? If I didn't go along with the plan, my only option would be to leave China entirely as soon as my student visa expired. The university wouldn't renew it since I wasn't a student anymore. Furthermore, I certainly didn't have the funds to afford a plane ticket home, and I was loath to leave the country. I told myself to just go along with Mr. Liu's plan, and before long, I'd have a shiny new work visa and all of China open to me.

Friday arrived quickly. I was exceedingly nervous, as this would be the first time I found myself in front of the police in China, and even though I was told that the officer was in on it, I still needed to make a good showing of pretending to have a broken leg. Mr. Liu held onto my left shoulder to support me as I hobbled to the officer's desk. I sat down in a cold, metal chair and extended my right foot out in front of me, rubbing my lower thigh as if I were in pain. The police officer gave me a brief look of concern before turning to Mr. Liu, who aimed to aid in translation.

"She can speak Chinese, but it isn't very good," he said. "Luckily, I can tell you everything that happened," he began. The officer cut him off.

"No," the officer responded gruffly, and brought his knuckles up to rest under his chin, "I want to hear it from her. I can understand just fine."

In truth, my Chinese was much better than I was letting on, but not being able to speak the language well was Mr. Liu's idea and I wanted to get everything right. I pulled out my phone and opened my translator app. I knew I'd need it anyway as I was still far from fluent.

"Well, you see, I fell down the stairs, and −" I started, but was promptly cut off.

"Where?" asked the officer.

"In my apartment," I replied

"In Tai'an?" he asked, and raised an eyebrow.

This was going to be problematic. I had come to China on a student visa that was tied specifically to Shandong University.

"But your visa was issued for Jinan," the officer continued on, "and here you are in Tai'An. You're not supposed to change cities without telling the police, you know, and what about your studies?"

"I'm so sorry," I said with a whimper, "I didn't know about that rule until it was too late."

That wasn't all a lie. I knew we had to register our addresses with the local police bureaus, but I thought since Jinan was still my main residence – and I still had an apartment in Jinan – I didn't need to worry about registering in Tai'an, too. Mr. Liu said it wasn't needed since the apartment was registered in his name. It all made sense in my head.

"So, you're in your apartment..." the police officer urged me to continue.

"Right, I was moving," I said.

"Moving in, or moving out?" the officer questioned sharply.

"Moving in," I replied, and continued, "And I had this real heavy box, you see, and well, I tripped over myself trying to go up the stairs and ended up falling down them. That's how I broke my leg."

The police officer stared at me in contemplation. He brought his hand back down to the desk and began to fidget with a pen. "So, why couldn't you leave the country?" he asked.

"The doctors told her not to," Mr. Liu interrupted on my behalf. "Here, I have all the paperwork."

With that, he handed over a stack of papers that documented when my accident had occurred, what treatment I'd received, which doctor had treated me, and the doctor's instructions to not board a plane for two months. These papers were all fake, of course, forged with the help of a professional Photoshop editor and a few generously greased palms at the small nearby hospital. Doctors in China don't make much money.

The officer thumbed through the paperwork, taking an occasional moment to glance my way. He pointed to my leg and said, "So you're all better now, ah?"

"Almost," I replied. "It still hurts. But I can fly on a plane now."

"Except your visa is expiring in two days, so unless you already have plane tickets bought for Monday, you can't leave without being massively fined," the officer said lowly as he looked me in the eyes. A small grin appeared on his face. I couldn't help but flinch.

"We're hoping you'll show us mercy," Mr. Liu hurried to chime in before I could speak. "She couldn't go home because of her health – it was an extenuating circumstance. She didn't mean any harm, and she's obviously not a bad person. Can't you help her out?"

"Fine," the officer sighed, and pulled out an official notepad from his desk, "but she'll have to write the whole story down on this. Then I'll need her fingerprints on the document to certify it. Then I'll see what I can do." With that, he stood up from his desk and walked out of the room, closing the door behind him. I turned to Mr. Liu.

"I thought you said he was in on it?" I asked.

"He is," he replied, "but he has to pretend like he isn't. Just to keep himself safe, too."

I leaned heavily on my translation app as I scribbled character after character onto the notepad, retelling the false story I'd rehearsed a dozen times. When I received my passport back from the police station a week later, I immediately flipped to the back to take in the sight of my new visa. It allowed me an extra two months. And it looked just like a real visa, too. I could barely tell it was a fake.

The visa granted me just enough time to finish out the spring semester at the high school. Mr. Liu continued to withhold my paychecks from me, citing visa expenses, and leaving me just enough to scrape by without too much complaining. I felt like I didn't have much recourse otherwise, since the police wouldn't be very sympathetic towards somebody already breaking the law. I kept my fake visa on the down-low and waited patiently for my work visa.

But it wouldn't be until a week before my fake visa expired that I learned that Mr. Liu had no intention of ever getting me a work visa. I called the school myself after constantly getting the run-around from everywhere else I turned, and the headmaster informed me that they'd told Mr. Liu when they initially hired me that they would not be willing to sponsor my work visa since I didn't meet the basic qualifications. Mr. Liu had been lying to me, and pocketing my paychecks for himself all the while. And now, I was at risk of deportation if I overstayed even my fake visa.

Anger seethed inside of me, and not just because Mr. Liu had duped me into his scam, but also because I fell for it all. I was some dumb nineteen-year-old who chalked everything up to "that's just how it works in China".

After finding this information out, I refused to return to Tai'An again. My students would have to find a new teacher for the last week of school, as I found myself marching down to the local police station in Jinan to get myself out of this pickle.

Suffice to say, Mr. Liu paid a massive 20,000 yuan fine for his actions, and I received a 2,000 yuan fine for being an idiot. I ended up flying home for the first time in over a year, but was back in China less than two months later, shiny new internship visa in my passport and a job at a private English training school waiting for me in Jinan. Over a decade later, I still have that Nokia phone.

The Foreign Haze

One of the most unexpected experiences in Jinan was the ease of scoring recreational drugs, if you knew where to look. Drugs didn't come in a wide variety, however, and one was mostly left to choose between marijuana, meth, or over-the-counter products that you couldn't get without a prescription back in Western society. Before coming to China, I'd been such a good girl. I'd never smoked a cigarette, let alone a joint, never went to a party, and I'd never gotten drunk. It wasn't that I wasn't interested in trying those things, I'd just never been afforded the opportunity and was too heavily focused on my studies with my peers. That all changed fairly quickly once I found myself in a place with easy access to debauchery.

The first time I got stoned in Jinan, I was with a group of men from Saudi Arabia. The Saudis had a reputation of coming to China loaded with cash, receiving a huge monthly stipend from the government, and spending it all on luxury items and lavish parties. Whether or not the Saudi guys in the group would be partaking in haram activities or keeping halal was about a fifty-fifty tossup. Many found that Jinan gave them the freedom to express themselves and experience as much "sin" as humanly possible before duty called them back to their homeland and they would have to lead what they considered to be boring lives. It always reminded me of the Amish rumspringa, exploring the world beyond their communities before deciding how they truly wanted to exist in it.

Abdullah was an old pro at living this life. He'd been at Shandong University for almost six years, well beyond the time he needed to earn a degree. Once he finished his Chinese Language courses, he decided to go into international relations at the same university, taking all his courses in Chinese. Abdullah was in his early thirties and was one of the oldest students on campus. He was friendly with everyone, regardless of race, religion, or nationality. He made fast friends with those outside of his immediate sphere of other Middle Easterners, and was eager to share in any way he could. Although largely unspoken, it was well known that Abdullah was safe for women to be around, too. He wouldn't sexualize you, harass you, or throw dog-whistles your way. He routinely steered too-drunk women away from his overly-eager Saudi friends who didn't always have the best intentions in mind, and he personally expressed to me that he wished there was more equality to be had for women.

So when Abdullah handed me a cigarette and said, "it's got weed in it," winking at me, I had little hesitation towards partaking. I'd started smoking cigarettes shortly after arriving in China. I got hooked on tobacco thanks to the numerous nights the Saudis would break out their shisha, passing around the nozzles to anyone who walked into the international student dorm's cafeteria lounge. One night, as the sky began to turn from black to quiet blue with the morning sun, we ran out of shisha. But a Lesotho girl had a pack of cigarettes, and as she passed them out to the known smokers, I asked for one too. From that day on I was hooked, and as it was considered customary to always take a cigarette when offered one in China, I certainly didn't want to be rude to Abdullah with his special treat.

"How did you get the weed inside the cigarette?" I asked after taking a long drag and choking on my first marijuana smoke.

"First you take out the tobacco," he explained. "Then you mix in the weed, then you stuff it all back inside." A grin swept across his face. "Clever, no?"

"Very," I responded, beginning to feel the effects. It didn't last long though, and there were three others also partaking in the spliff. We managed to pass it around the circle twice.

As the group was splitting for the night, I walked with Abdullah up the dormitory stairs. "Do you think I could buy some of that weed from you?" I asked. I'd heard that the Saudis were the ones to turn to for anything marijuana related, but I'd never asked about it directly before this.

"Absolutely!" Abdullah said, patting my shoulder. "Just give me a day or two. It's 200 *kuai*, okay?"

I agreed to the price. 200 *kuai* (the conversational word for dollar) was less than 25 dollars American. I wasn't sure how much weed cost in the States, and I wasn't sure how much I'd be getting, but it seemed like a fair enough deal. I always imagined myself being a stoner after growing up with old hippie parents (although I was a very straight-laced kid before coming to China), and if I had my own weed, I could mix it in with my cigarettes and learn how to actually get high. Then I could share with my friends too, I thought.

Two days later Abdullah knocked on my dorm room door, smiling his signature ear-to-ear grin. "I have a present for you," he declared as I ushered him into my room. He handed me a big ball of something, wrapped in a red plastic bag and tied with twine.

"Make sure you keep it hidden, okay? Don't just leave it out on your desk. We don't want the *Ayi's* finding out," he said. *Ayi*, or auntie, was the polite way of addressing the cleaning ladies that tended to the dorms, maintaining the halls and lounges. We didn't have to worry too much – few Chinese people knew what marijuana smelled like, let alone what it looked like – but erring on the side of caution was always a good idea. Not every student in the dormitory was okay with illegal activities, either. If you were Chinese and got caught with weed, you were looking at a five-year jail sentence. If you were a foreigner, it was immediate deportation. Unless you had the money to "pay it off".

He started unwrapping the bag as I collected the 200 *kuai* to give to him. As I handed the money over, I noticed that the content of the bag was not what I imagined a bud of marijuana would look like, but rather a heaping pile of fine, green powder. "What is that?" I asked with a look of confusion on my face.

"Oh, it's kief!" Abdhulla explained. "It's just as good as a flower, and I like it better. It doesn't take as much to get high and it's much cheaper. Don't worry, you'll be all good with this, okay? There's a full ounce here."

I thanked Abdhulla and handed him the money. He grinned again and patted my shoulder before making his way out of my room. I stood over my desk, staring at the powder. It really was a lot of kief. I immediately took out my pack of cigarettes and a pair of tweezers. Emptying the tobacco contents on a scrap piece of paper on the desk, I mixed in a pinch of kief. Then another. Then a third for good measure. But packing the mixture back in the cigarette tube proved to be quite the feat that involved the use of a pencil, a tiny straw, and one of my last q-tips. I made three of these spliffs and neatly tucked them back away in my pack of cigarettes before retying the little red bundle and placing it in my nightstand.

That night, I shared a spliff with my friends on the steps in front of the dormitory entrance. I didn't pack the spliffs very well, and the cherries kept falling off, but overall they got the job done and had the lot of us mildly high. Abdhulla found us later and asked how we were doing. I told him about my struggles with the tobacco, and he chuckled. "I'll show you the real way to do it," he said smiling. "Wait here".

He returned with an empty liter bottle, some tin foil, a pair of scissors, and a mechanical pencil. We gathered around him as we watched him remove the cap from the bottle, tear off a small square of foil, and wrap the foil around the mouth of the bottle, creating a small bowl at the top. Then he took the mechanical pencil and poked tiny holes in the foil bowl. He then proceeded to take apart the mechanical pencil, leaving just the hollow outer shell. Then, taking the scissors, he stabbed one hole in the middle of the bottle, and another hole halfway around the other side. He slid the mechanical pencil into the back hole and held up the contraption.

"Did you see how I made that?" he asked. "Simple, anyone can do it. Now let's see your tobacco." I handed him a cigarette, and he tore open the end, exposing the tobacco leaves.

"Just take a pinch like this and put it in the bottom of the bowl you made at the top," he explained, gently tapping the tobacco down with a finger.

"That will keep the kief from spilling into the hole. Then, just add as much as you want on top. Light it and breathe in the smoke through the pencil, like this." He demonstrated lighting and inhaling.

"The other hole over here is to get all the smoke in. I forget the name for it in English. But you know how to work it," he said as the group nodded "yes" to his statement.

"You can even put a little water in the bottom if you like, that makes it more like a bong," he said as he handed me the contraption. "You can keep this one, but don't use it more than once or twice, or else it gets nasty."

Of course, we all had to try this clever makeshift smoking device right away. We all shuffled into my dorm room, and someone placed a towel in front of the crack at the bottom of the door to keep the smoke and smell from rolling out. It was easy to disguise your weed as a cigarette in public, but another thing entirely to just use a bong out in the open, so we again erred on the side of caution. The level of high we achieved was enough for me to decide that this was the only method I'd be using going forward.

Two weeks later, four friends and I decided to hike up to the top of Thousand Buddha Mountain, a small mountain with a peak 935 feet above sea level, famous for its hundreds of Buddhas erected along the mountain's footpaths, inside the mountain's cave, and carved in the mountain's faces. The trek to the top took about two hours, but properly exploring the area could easily add another three. While passing by some wild flora, we noticed a particularly interesting patch of plants. We squinted, unsure of what we were actually seeing.

"Is that...?" asked one friend.

"Oh, it definitely is," responded another.

A huge patch of marijuana grew tall and proud, not twenty feet away from the rocky path. It was truly the definition of ditch weed, but we found a handful of female plants with nicely formed buds and collected our bounty. Nobody said a word as they passed us. Few people even glanced. The vast majority of local Jinaners just didn't know how to identify marijuana. They had no access to education on the topic, and most assumed marijuana would make you go crazy, comparing it to cocaine. On the way down the mountain, an old lady stopped us, pointing at the weed.

"I have that in my windowsill!" she exclaimed. "I think it's lovely!" We all agreed that it was a lovely plant indeed, and smiled at each other as we continued on our ways.

We let the ditch weed dry in our rooms for a week. We had no clue what we were doing, and our internet searches were fruitless and government monitored. Eventually, we all piled into a dorm room, rolled the flower into cigarettes, and tried so desperately to get high. We failed miserably.

We weren't the only ones to experience the thrill of finding wild weed in Jinan, however. A couple years later, a fresh coworker for an English training school I worked for went to Thousand Buddha Mountain alone and returned with a large armful of weed bundled up under his elbow.

"I found weed!" he exclaimed joyfully. "There's so much of it! And nobody even looked at me when I was picking it!"

I warned him about my prior experience, but he shrugged it off. The next weekend, he invited me over to his apartment to smoke with him. When I arrived, the apartment was completely filled with smoke, the weed plants smoldering in a large metal bowl in the middle of the living room floor.

"What in the world is going on?" I asked, trying not to choke on the air.

"I was too impatient to wait, so I decided to just burn everything and make one giant hotbox in my apartment," he explained, thinking he was very clever.

But the smile on his face quickly dropped. "I think they're all male plants, though." He coughed. "I don't feel a thing."

I stayed for as long as I could in the smoke-filled apartment, opening windows to vent the smoke and resisting the urge to call my friend an idiot. It was a good experiment, I supposed. As I've said, none of us really knew what we were doing.

When I changed universities and started working full time, I decided to rent my own apartment. Living in an apartment meant that I could buy a small countertop oven for baking. Ovens aren't considered a necessary appliance in China, and finding one small enough to fit on the counter while still being large enough to handle a half sheet pan was a struggle. But after a month of searching, I found the perfect little oven to cater to my baking needs.

I was still buying kief from the Saudis, despite not attending Shandong University for two years at that point. I was now attending Shandong Normal University, a teacher's college, and would regularly lounge in the dorm rooms of my friends after class, crafting a makeshift bong with a plastic bottle and tin foil for everyone to share.

After buying my oven, I decided to try my hand at making edibles. I thought brownies would be the perfect delicacy to test my lack-of-skills on. Connecting to the internet through a VPN, I was able to find a guide on how to create cannabutter, and how to use that butter to make brownies. I followed the directions to a T, melting the butter in a double boiler before adding in the kief and stirring, stirring, slowly, slowly, for over an hour until everything was well incorporated and the fat had completely soaked into the kief. The only thing that was missing, however, was how much butter to use. The brownie recipe called for ten tablespoons of butter, so I substituted all ten tablespoons with cannabutter.

The brownies reeked of marijuana when they came out of the oven. I figured that was typical – they were *weed brownies* after all – and cut them neatly into nine individual squares. I called my friend, Samm, to let her know that I was on my way to her dorm room with brownies in hand, and to gather all the girls to test out my baking. By the time I arrived, five of my closest female friends were sprawled across the dorm room, eagerly awaiting my arrival. We all had a brownie.

And nothing happened. None of us had ever done edibles before, and after forty minutes of waiting for the high to kick in, I was feeling disappointed that my experiment had failed. They didn't even taste good, but rather like someone had dipped a joint in chocolate powder and passed it off as a baked good. I sighed. "Maybe we need to eat more?" I suggested.

"I'll have another one if you do," responded one American friend.

"I'd rather just smoke, ya know?" chimed in our British companion.

My American friend and I gobbled down another brownie, mostly out of spite, and afterwards I turned an empty large water bottle into a bong contraption for the rest of the group. They partook liberally. I joined in for two rounds.

With no exaggeration, I began getting violently high immediately after smoking the second round. The brownies were finally kicking in, and I had not one, but two on board, plus a couple of hits from the bong. I felt myself begin to melt into the floor as my lips widened in an involuntary smile. I looked around the room, and saw the rest of my friends doing the same.

"I'm well smashed…" our British friend said, very slowly. I saw her try to get up from the bed. She managed to get her feet on the ground with her arms supporting her on the bed as she tried to push her way up to a standing position, but it was no use. She slowly sank back down to the bed, mumbling, "I'm not going anywhere."

A knock on the door came unexpectedly. Our flamboyantly

gay Eritrean friend had come to visit, hearing of our plans to get high. His jaw dropped and his eyes blinked furiously at us when he saw our collective conditions.

"What did you eat?" he asked us, chuckling. "Everyone's eyes are so red, Habibi!"

"I… I made brownies. Do… do you want some?" I offered him the pan of treats. He put up a hand and laughed.

"Not if it's going to make me be like THIS!" he said, sweeping his hand across the lot of us. "You girls are too much!"

The truth is, we hadn't even begun to know the meaning of the word "stoned" yet, at least when it came to these brownies. In retrospect, I should have only replaced less than half of the real butter with the cannabutter. Instead, I'd mixed it all in, essentially doubling the dose for everyone involved.

"You… have… to get off… my bed… now, please," our American friend blurted out as best she could. "It's not that… I don't… like you… I just can't… handle… people on my… bed right now," she managed.

Those of us that were on her bed in any capacity slowly creeped away from it, finding new spots on the hard tile floor. We sat in silence until somebody started laughing. Then we *all* found laughing to be very funny indeed, and soon each of us were laughing with tears in our eyes at absolutely nothing at all.

I decided to try and make my way to the desk by the window. It was maybe ten feet from the floor to the desk chair, but I wasn't certain I could make it that far. I asked my friends to time me. It took me four minutes and forty-five seconds to make it over the distance, but once I found myself sitting at the desk, I felt a lot less high. Or at least I was feeling more cognitive. I looked out the window and saw a most welcome sight – Micah, another American who was also navigating life in Jinan as both a full-time teacher and a full-time student, was rolling up to the international student dormitory gates on his electric bike.

Micah was no stranger to getting high. In fact, one of the first times I actually sat down and spoke to Micah was while passing around a joint in Hulu Bar, whose owner was an aficionado for cannabis and reggae, and who would later be imprisoned for marijuana use. I slid the dorm window open and hollered for him to join us.

"This smells like trouble!" he hollered back.

It took a couple of minutes for Micah to make his way to the dorm room and find an empty spot on a bed. He declined a brownie, but accepted the bong.

"Don't you have to work today?" Micah asked me, coughing on smoke.

"Not today!" I yipped. "I'm not brave enough for that."

While we had friends who would time their edibles to kick in right as classes were ending, I knew I didn't want to be in the classroom high. It had happened to me once – I smoked before work and went into the classroom high as a kite. But while singing silly songs and reading five letter words was all great fun while stoned, the paranoia that the parents would be able to tell you're high and get you fired was slightly terrifying.

"Pussy Dragon Day would have been a lot more humorous if I were high, though," I added.

Micah chortled, "What's a pussy dragon?"

Very slowly and with much focus, I told the group the story about teaching my Tai'An students how to curse, and how all of them incorrectly used the word "pussy" to describe a dragon. Tears were streaming down my face in laughter by the time I described how mad I was while grading all those stories, and how everyone featured a "very pussy dragon".

"What would a pussy dragon even look like?" laughed our Slovakian friend.

And so, we drew. A great tubular oval with a slightly triangular shape, wings sprouting from the side, three rows of razor-sharp teeth and an acid spray in place of fire. It had hair in place of scales, and we decided it required no feet. The pussy dragon had taken on a new form of life, now, and we were howling in delight.

Micah stayed with us until we started getting hungry. By then, it was early evening. "I need to go home," he said. "And you all need to get something to eat, too, it's already dinner time."

We all fumbled around to find our phones, gasping at the time. My stomach cried out to be fed, but I was dismayed knowing that my refrigerator at home was empty. I was in no condition to be cooking, either, which meant that eating out would be the way to go. I considered my options as I said goodbye to my friends and stumbled out of the dorms.

I decided a sandwich sounded delicious. Two sandwich shops were close to the university, and it had been weeks since I'd had Western food. The first shop, Heisenberg's, was just a small shop front in a hole in the wall plastered with Walter White's face and Breaking Bad pictures. They sold eight-inch sandwiches for 20 kuai. Or, you could pay with bitcoin. A Grecian friend once paid for his sandwich with his sole bitcoin in 2012. He now remarks it was the most expensive sandwich he ever bought.

Aside from Heisenberg's was Subway, which was closer than Heisenberg's, but more expensive. Still, the prospect of a tuna sandwich with hot, melted cheese sounded very enticing, and I'd have enough to save for two meals if I ordered a footlong. So, Subway it was. I rehearsed my order in my head as I walked through the door and stood in line. I wanted to get the Chinese just right, and this was going to be a mouthful to order.

"I'd like a footlong tuna on wheat bread with cheese, toasted, please," I told the counter worker. I smiled to myself knowing I'd gotten all the words correct. The worker asked me what toppings I'd like.

"Lettuce, cucumber, pickles, and black olives," I replied.

He stared at me blankly. Then repeated himself, "What would you like on it?"

I repeated myself, "Lettuce, cucumber, pickles, black olives."

"Miss," he said, waving a hand, "excuse me, but would you like anything on top of your sandwich?"

It was then that I realized I hadn't actually been speaking when I replied to him. Rather, I was having my end of the conversation all in my head. The cables between *thinking* what I wanted to say and actually speaking it out loud were disconnected. I apologized profusely, used my words the right way, and walked out of the shop with a sandwich in one hand and a dozen extra cookies I hadn't planned for (but couldn't resist) in the other.

We were regularly stoned in Jinan, gifting each other weed-related goodies for Christmases and birthdays, and while marijuana may have been my drug of choice, it wasn't the only drug available.

"I've been doing some research," my American friend, Katherine, told me one day during Chinese New Year, "and you can get dextromethorphan over the counter here."

"What's dextromethorphan?" I asked, completely oblivious. I had been staying with Katherine for a few days over the holiday while our other friends were all away on vacation.

"It's the active ingredient in cough syrup, DXM," she explained, "and if you drink enough of it, it'll get you high. I already tried it last week, actually, but I want to do it again."

"What's it like?" I asked excitedly.

"Very artsy," she replied, and showed me the vibrant color drawings from her sketch pad.

"Oh, I am so down for that," I told her, and we began to make plans.

Katherine loaded the website she'd found that described the proper way to dose based on body weight. She would only need two bottles, but I would need three or four. We both decided I should start with three, but we'd buy four for me just in case. And with that, we headed towards the closest pharmacy. The streets and shops were practically empty, with everyone gone back to their hometowns to ring in the Spring Festival with their families. In truth, we were lucky that the pharmacies were still open too.

Katherine looked around the shop, poking at boxes and turning over bottles, trying to find the Chinese characters for dextromethorphan that I'd written on a piece of paper for reference. A few moments of doing the same made me realize things might go faster if I'd just asked the pharmacist, who led us to a large display with three different brands of pure DXM. We grabbed our six bottles, paid, and scurried out of the pharmacy as if we'd just done something wrong. The pharmacists didn't care, though. You could buy as much as you wanted since it wasn't a controlled substance. We stopped at the neighboring convenience store for water, which was vital in a country with unsafe tap water, and snacks, which we anticipated being vital on our upcoming journey.

Back at Katherine's apartment, we broke the seals off our bottles and chugged. Where I had been expecting a thick, difficult syrup was a thin and sweet-tasting liquid. It was like drinking candy. An hour later, I was filled with both euphoria and energy, and Katherine put me to work creating art on her living room floor. The music that played on her laptop made the colors around me vibrate, and we spent what felt like an entire night trapped in a 90-minute movie. It was well past midnight when we decided to sleep, exhausted from our trip, and we were both pleased to find that we awoke the next morning feeling like there was a bit more spring in our steps.

With most shops and centers closed for the holiday, Katherine and I spent the afternoon lazing about her apartment, tidying up from the night before and wondering what sort of trouble we could get up to next. Then I received a text from Jackie.

"*What are you doing, Anna?*" his message read.

Then another, "*Are you in Jinan for the holiday?*"

Jackie was my ex-boyfriend. He was a Hui Muslim man who drank, smoke, danced, and engaged in premarital sex, all the things a young Muslim man from Qinghai was supposed to avoid at all costs. Our relationship only lasted a couple of months, breaking up after he cheated on me with a sixteen-year-old girl. She was well past the age of consent in China, but I was both disgusted that someone his age would go after a teenager and angry with myself for falling in with a playboy. But somehow, Jackie and I remained friends over the years. I think neither of us wanted to let go of the novelty of each other, him being an ethnic minority from a faraway land and me being a foreigner from just a little farther away.

"*Yeah, I'm in Jinan with my friend Katherine,*" I responded.

"*Can I come over?*" he typed in response.

I ran the idea past Katherine. She had no issue with his presence, so I texted Jackie the address. It would make for an interesting night, since Katherine spoke very little Chinese and Jackie spoke no English. Then I had an idea.

"Katherine, we need to get Jackie high," I said.

"Is he down for that?" she questioned.

"I don't really know, to be honest," I said. "I think he'll want to do it. We can at least ask."

Jackie *did* want to do it. When he arrived at Katherine's apartment, I told him about our previous night. When I told him that I wanted him to try it, too, he became visibly excited. He smiled wide, nodding his head and drumming his palms on his knees.

"Okay, let's do it! Do we do it now?" he asked.

"We have to go to the pharmacy first," I responded.

"Oh, that might be a problem," Jackie said. "Most of the pharmacies are closed today since it's so close to the New Year. I know the one by Pizza Hut is still open, but I think it closes tonight at 6pm."

I translated for Katherine, and we decided that Jackie and I would head to the pharmacy right away, and pick up a pizza on our way home. Pizza Hut in China was considered fine dining. The pizzas were thick, loaded with stringy cheese and plenty of toppings. Everything felt fresh and delicate. You put on your nice clothes to eat at Pizza Hut, and you paid good money, too. And although you couldn't customize your pizzas, we found that corn and pepperoni actually make an enticing couple.

We decided to order the pizza first and make our way to the pharmacy while it was cooking. We purchased eighteen bottles of DXM, leaving all but two bottles behind on the display table. Three for each of us, and enough for two days. Jackie paid. Then we picked up the pizza. Jackie paid. Then we hailed a taxi back to Katherine's apartment. Again, Jackie paid.

Knowing Jackie, I could tell that something was wrong. He

got generous when he was sad, and this was the first time in months he'd asked to hang out. It was also the first time since we'd broken up that he didn't bring along another friend or three.

"Are you okay?" I asked him, but he brushed me off with a wave of his hand.

"I'm fine," he said. "I just have a lot to think about."

Silence filled the taxi before he turned to me again to say, "Thank you for letting me chill with you."

Back at Katherine's apartment, we put the pizza aside and cracked open our bottles of cough suppressant. We toasted one another, then chugged. We were all smokers, and smoking in your apartment was common in China, so we all lit up from Jackie's cigarettes as we waited for the effects to kick in. In China, it's rude to refuse your friend's cigarettes, and since Jackie was the guest, he was the first to offer his. We all knew that by the end of the night we'd be sharing all our packs between the three of us, and luckily smokes were cheap and easy to come by.

Katherine put on the movie Pitch Perfect and Jackie watched in delight as we sang and danced to the songs. I then pulled out Katherine's art supplies and scattered them in front of Jackie.

"What should I make?" he asked, pupils dilated so wide they took up his entire face.

"Whatever you feel, man," I said, and watched him take a piece of watercolor paper and paints. I watched him for over an hour as he sketched out then colored in a bright red iris flower. I had no idea he could create like that. He said he didn't know he could do that, either.

"Each color has a different feeling," he said, "like they're each trying to tell me something different. So, I made it into a picture." He was beaming with pride.

"I don't know about you all, but I'm ready to really get this party started," Katherine said, and disappeared into her room.

She came back with a bag of kief and an opium pipe in the shape of a little kettle. It was a genius find that kept her from needing to manufacture a makeshift bong every time she wanted to smoke. Instead, she would line the pipe with a sprig of tobacco and pack it with the kief. It worked way better than an apple and was a lot less prone to toppling over than a plastic bottle. She packed a bowl, took a hit, then handed me the pipe.

"It's marijuana," I told Jackie, then inhaled deeply on the pipe, choking on the smoke as I let it out.

"I want to try it," he said a bit hesitantly. "Will it make me crazy?"

"No," I chuckled. There was copious misinformation about weed in China. "It'll just make you feel relaxed. And everything will be funny."

We spent a couple of minutes showing Jackie how to use the pipe, teaching him how to take a hit, and warning him that he would probably cough, but not to worry, that was necessary. As he took his first hit, I couldn't help but think of the Korean classmate I'd gotten stoned at my recent birthday party. It was his first time smoking marijuana, and he'd had such a bad trip, he got lost between a bed and a windowsill and couldn't move. He had to be escorted back to his dorm room before we even made it to cake. I wondered if Jackie's first time would be similar.

We passed the pipe around our little circle until the kief was just ash. I watched as a small grin crept across Jackie's face, which then turned into a big, toothy smile as he slumped down into the couch.

"Let's watch something funny," Katherine said, and found a standup routine for us to watch. Jackie couldn't understand a word of what was said, but he thought it was funny when we laughed. So, he laughed at us laughing, and we laughed a lot.

Before long, it was midnight again. And then 1am. And then 2am. And Jackie was still at the apartment. By the time 4am rolled around, we realized that Jackie wasn't planning on going home. He wasn't in any state to leave, anyway. We'd been smoking weed all night, and his family couldn't see him like this. We made him a bed up on the couch where he curled up with all his clothes and jewelry still on.

Jackie stayed the whole next day, as well. It felt too awkward to ask him to leave, and by now even Katherine could tell that something was up with him, so we decided to just let him be where he wanted to be. He left the apartment twice in between more bottles of DXM and the kief to find us food, drink, and smokes. He came back with a case of beer and a bottle of baijiu the second time, and we partied harder than the previous night.

As this night drew to a close, though, Jackie turned to me with sadness in his eyes.

"I'm never going to be able to do this again, you know," he said.

"I know," I responded.

"My friends would never do this with me," he said.

"I know," I responded.

"This was the best time of my life, my brain has been opened, and I'm never going to get to do it again, am I?" he questioned.

"I mean… it's up to you, really." I said. But we both knew that in reality, Jackie was never going to get high on DXM or marijuana without foreigners to hide behind. Many of our Chinese friends were comfortable doing drugs with us, but never on their own or with their local friends. It was as though we created a comfort shield, and that was okay.

I didn't feel bad for him, though. In fact, I was a little pleased by his situation. I didn't hate Jackie, but I still held some resentment towards him. I was rather happy to know that I'd given him this life altering experience, and happier still to look at it as getting my bit of vengeance for cheating. "He'll never have this experience again," I thought to myself, "and that's exactly what I want. Look at what you're missing, friend." I wasn't beyond being petty on the inside.

I fell asleep with Jackie on the couch that night. We had stayed up much later than Katherine, and adding alcohol into the mix just made our eyelids heavy. Jackie's chainsaw snoring woke me up, moving me back to the spare bedroom. By the time I woke up the next afternoon, Katherine and Jackie were both up and chatting awkwardly on the sofa, each one trying to conjure up sentences in the other's language.

"I was waiting for you to wake up before I said goodbye," Jackie said, standing up and pulling on his black leather jacket. "Really, Anna, thanks for everything." He hugged us both goodbye, something I'd taught him to do with foreign friends, then he left.

I never did find out what demons Jackie was chasing. But I'm glad he got a couple nights of being high to help work it out of his system.

What Happened in Qingdao

The third time I found myself in front of the police in China, I was fighting for my life. I had run into a Uni-Mart, China's favorite chain of convenience stores, shaking as I looked over my shoulder.

"Please, you've gotta help me," I panted frantically at the cashier. "Call the police!"

She stared at me in shock, unmoving.

"PLEASE!" I begged. "He's coming!" Of all the experiences I was expecting to have on our vacation to the seaside city of Qingdao this was certainly not on my list.

The day had started benignly. My good friend, Maxine, who was both rich and lonely, invited me on a weekend getaway trip to the coast. The train ride from Jinan to Qingdao was only three hours, and Maxine had made plans to stay in an old observatory-turned-hostel. The hostel itself was renowned for its bar and balcony, positioned where a giant telescope once stood. We'd had a fine meal and shared a bottle of wine, and as the evening turned dark we made plans to tour the Qingdao nightlife.

We hailed a taxi.

"Take us to a bar," we said cheerfully, climbing inside.

"Which bar?" the driver asked.

"Any bar!" I replied. "Whichever bar you think is the best."

And with that, we were off. I expected the driver to tote us around the city for a while, going out of his way to heighten our cab fare and taking advantage of the fact that we knew nothing about the area. But to my pleasant surprise, we were in the car for less than ten minutes before the driver pulled up to a giant two-story bar. We happily paid our fare and practically skipped inside. We were eager for the night to *really* begin.

Sitting at the bar, Maxine pulled a foil pill pack out of her purse. She was an addict, and her drug of choice was sleeping pills. They weren't the kind of pills that made you fall asleep, but rather the scary kinds that just "assisted" with the sleep process, and had a reputation for causing the user to do things like sleep-walk and sleep-kill. But if you could push past the initial wave of sleepiness, the pills would get you high instead of making you walk unknowingly into traffic or stab your sleeping partner. Maxine regularly took ten at a time, and washed them down with the liquor of her choice. She began popping them out of the blister pack one by one.

"Give me one," I said, and stretched an open palm out in her direction.

"No way," Maxine responded. "You'll get way too messed up."

"No, I won't," I insisted, "I just want to know what it's like. I'm curious about your experience."

"Fine," she replied, smiling, "but you're only getting half." She broke a pill in half with her teeth and handed me the larger piece. Then she bought us a round of beer.

I still can't remember what time the sleeping pill kicked in, nor do I remember losing Maxine, but suddenly I was alone at the bar. I was high, but the world felt droopy, and my extremities were the heaviest they'd ever been. A stranger was talking at me, teeth and lips and tongue all working hard to tell me a story that I just couldn't hear over the boom of the music. I smiled and nodded and reached for what I assumed was my beer. I saw the bartender place two shot glasses in front of the stranger, pouring an alcohol I couldn't make out. The stranger slid a shot glass over to me, and I threw it to the back of my throat. Tequila.

The next thing I remembered, the lights in the bar were all turned on. It was closing time, and the bartender was busy wiping down his counter while the assistants shuffled around the bar room tables, sweeping and cleaning. The stranger was still next to me, but we were the only two patrons left.

"Come on, I'll take you back to your hostel," he said.

"But, I… I don't know how to get there…" I stammered, "and I… I need to get my friend. Do you know wh… where she is?"

"Oh, she left already with that guy," he chuckled. "Yeah, they were going to have a good time."

Then he continued, "And don't worry, I know the way back to your place. C'mon, I'll save you the cab fare."

Between the pills and the beer, I was drunk and high and stupid enough to get in his van. As we traveled through the city streets, I had a suspicion that we weren't going back to my hostel. The drive had only lasted ten minutes in the taxi, and we'd already been driving for at least that long. The stranger was silent now, but smiling. Suddenly, he turned to me.

"Hey, my friends are really going to love meeting you, ah!" he said.

"What do you mean?" I asked, trying to parse through what he'd just said. "What friends? We're just going back to the hostel."

"No," he replied, still smiling, "I'm taking you to my place. That's where my friends are. And they're going to get to know you a little."

My eyes grew wide as I felt my heart drop to my stomach. I

did not want to go back to this man's place, and I certainly didn't want to know what his friends had planned for me. My palms grew sweaty as I scanned around the interior of the van. I still had my purse. Okay, good. And my phone. Even better. But it was dead. So maybe not better. And I had my smokes... wait, that's it! Smokes!

A Uni-Mart was just ahead and close enough to the upcoming stoplight that I decided to make a break for it as soon as we slowed. I quietly placed my hand on the door handle and slid over in my seat. When the van slowed for the red light, I loudly blurted out, "I have to buy more cigarettes!" Then I threw open the car door and pushed myself out as fast as I could. I bolted for the convenience store, bursting through the wide strips of plastic that hung in the doorway to keep the night air at bay.

"You've gotta help me!" I screamed at the cashier, but it was as though my pleas for assistance had gone in one ear and out the other. She didn't call for help. Bystanders in China just don't help others in trouble. So, when I saw the stranger pushing his own way past the plastic, I screamed and ran behind a display. He followed me, striding through the store in my direction.

"Call the police!" I cried again and again. "He's going to hurt me!"

The cashiers were screaming at us both to leave. They weren't going to help. The stranger grabbed at me, and his fingers caught my shirt. I pushed a display of drinks over in front of him to stop him from coming closer. He bared his teeth in anger.

"Come here!" he snarled, and lunged at me.

It felt as though we were playing this game of cat-and-mouse for an eternity. Luckily, just as I'd turned my attention to finding something to use as a weapon, two police officers pushed their way into the door. The man stopped immediately upon seeing the police. The officers approached us and demanded to know what was happening.

I ran up to the officers, positioning them between myself and the stranger. I pleaded with them, "He's trying to kidnap me, please help me!" The man took a step closer, breathing in deep as if he were preparing to shout. I stepped forward towards the officer until my body touched his arm. The officer held out a hand to stop the stranger and gently pushed me away from him.

"You're both coming to the police station," he said. "In separate cars."

We arrived at the station at 3:17 am. I remember seeing the big white clock ticking away on the wall. We were both led past the main lobby and into the back office area, the stranger ushered into a separate room while I sat in a cubicle in the middle of the station. I was by myself for quite some time, and I tried to get my body to sober up. But my mind was dragging, my limbs were heavy, and I was out of breath. I was in desperate need of water too, as my tongue stuck to the roof of my mouth, tacky with drying saliva.

Eventually, the officer returned to his cubicle.

"I need to see your passport," he said. I handed him my passport. Foreigners were to keep their passports on them at all times while traveling, and mine was tucked neatly in my purse. He flipped through the book, scrutinizing every visa and border stamp.

"What are you doing in Qingdao?" he asked me, still looking through my passport.

"I'm here with my friend, we're just having a weekend trip," I answered.

"And where is your friend now?" he asked, looking up at me.

"I don't know," I admitted. "I lost her at the bar."

"You're here as a student?" he asked, and held up the page with my latest student visa.

"Yes," I said, "at Shandong Normal University." I left out the fact that I was also working illegally as an English teacher when I wasn't in class. If the police found out, they would have me deported....

The officer sat my passport down on his desk and turned to his computer. He began typing. And typing. And typing. I sat swaying in his cubicle, feeling a beast of a hangover begin to set in. I thumbed around in my purse, trying to occupy myself, and landed on my pack of cigarettes. I had two left.

"Can I... can I go smoke a cigarette?" I asked the officer.

He looked at me in hesitation. Smoking was a common hobby in China, and he looked like he could use one, too. But he answered with a slow, "no", then went back to typing.

Then he stopped. He turned to me, saying, "I need you to tell me everything that happened. I'm going to type it up."

I told him about the hostel, the taxi driver, the bar, and conveniently left out the part about taking drugs. I told him that I'd gotten too drunk, and couldn't find my friend when it was time to leave, that this stranger had offered to take me home, but in truth he had other intentions. After recalling the night's events, I sat in silence, listening to the clacking of the keyboard. Then the officer stood up and left his cubicle, heading for the room that housed the stranger.

He returned an hour later.

"You're free to go," he told me.

"What about that guy?" I asked, pointing to the room with the stranger.

"Well, he gave us a false name at first. And he wouldn't tell us why he's in Qingdao. When we searched him, we found his identity card. But it had a different name on it, and his address is listed as being in Hong Kong."

"Hong Kong!" I said with a gasp.

"We're going to do a lot more investigation on him, but you're not needed here anymore," said the officer. And he motioned for me to follow him to the front door of the building.

"Is there any way I could get a ride back to the hostel?" I asked. "I don't know the address and I don't have enough money for cab fare. My phone is dead, too, so I can't call anyone."

"You're on your own for that one," the officer responded as he held the door open for me.

A solid twenty minutes passed before I could find a cab that would sympathize with my situation and work with me to figure out where I was supposed to go. My purse had less than ten yuan left, but that, a good story, and a shared cigarette were enough to get me back to the hostel. When I arrived back at our room, the door was locked, so I knew Maxine was inside. She finally woke up and let me in after banging on the door for fifteen minutes. The first thing I did when I was finally safe inside was slump to the floor and cry.

Maxine crawled back into bed, not bothering to ask where I'd been all night. It would take her half the day to recover from all that Lunesta. As I watched her chest slowly rise and fall as if all was right with the world, I decided that was both my first and last experiment with sleeping pills.

No Turkeys in China

My apple-head Siamese cat, Phoebe, meowed loudly at me as I picked her up and carried her to the sunroom. Her bent tail swished back and forth as I placed her on the tile counter, next to my orange and white kitten, Midas.

"I can't have you two getting underfoot right now," I told them both as Midas tried once again to escape the confines of the sunroom.

"I'm going to be moving everything around!" I tried to explain.

Phoebe meowed in protest and Midas scratched at the still-closed door. I felt bad about locking them away, but I was preparing to move literally every piece of furniture in my apartment, and the last thing I needed was to trip over one of them, or worse.

It was November of my third year in Jinan, and feeling homesick as America's holiday season started, I decided to host a Thanksgiving dinner at my house. Thanksgiving in China was hit and miss with only a handful of Americans in the city, meaning it went largely overlooked. So, when I invited all my classmates and fellow English teachers over to my house to celebrate, I greatly underestimated the amount of interest it would generate. My latest headcount sat at eighteen people, and my apartment was only 775 square feet. Needless to say, I was worried about space.

My apartment was considered old. Built in the early 1980s, the building was made entirely out of concrete, including the walls and floors. The six-story building had no elevator, but luckily I was only on the second floor. Walking into the apartment, the first thing one saw was the living room. It was exceedingly small, however, with space for two small futon couches and a coffee table. Between the two couches and the table was enough space for a pair of legs to sit comfortably, and if I didn't mind my back pressed up against a futon, I could just fit into the space between the couch and the coffee table, sitting on the floor. The kitchen and bathroom sat to the left of the living room. The kitchen was double the size of the living room and full of shelves and cabinets. I had a double-sink, a full-size stove top, a refrigerator, and about four feet of extra counter space. The bathroom was long and narrow, with the toilet at the back of the room on a small, elevated platform that separated it from the shower area. The bathroom came equipped with a western toilet instead of a squatty-potty, which made me lucky, and I was luckier still that my toilet paper stayed dry when the shower was on. In China, showers aren't separate entities, and toilets often get wet while bathing. Two bedrooms sat to the right of the living room. Equal in size, they were the largest rooms of the house. The master bedroom was also attached to the sunroom, meant for hanging clothes to dry and bathing plants in light. Each bedroom had a queen-sized bed, a large wardrobe, and a desk. Somehow, I would need to rearrange all of this to accommodate my guests.

I started in the master bedroom by shoving the bed as close to the corner of the back wall as possible. Then I dragged in the orange futon from the living room and placed it flat against my large wardrobe. Then I carried in the matching orange glass coffee table and placed it in between the futon and the bed. I placed a couple of ashtrays on the coffee table and another on my writing desk. This would be the designated smoking room. At least half of the people who were coming were smokers, including myself, and stepping outside to smoke was unheard of.

I repeated this performance in the other bedroom, pushing the bed against the wall and dragging the second beige futon in front of the wardrobe. Three people could fit on each futon, and at least three more people could claim a seat on a bed. I still didn't have enough seating for the rest of my guests, but my living room was now just bare floor. The previous owners had laid down tile flooring on top of the concrete, so at least it looked nice, but I couldn't have guests just sitting on the cold, hard tile. I moved to my wardrobe, grabbed four blankets, and proceeded to lay them out flat on the living room floor. Then I gathered up all of my throw pillows, bedroom pillows, and large stuffed animals and placed them around the edges of the living room, providing cushions for the blanket-on-the-floor seating area. It would have to do. It looked a bit odd, but you could clearly tell the area was meant for sitting, so I left it as it was.

At this point, I had to get cooking. I'd asked everyone to bring either a dish or a beverage to share, but since I was hosting, I wanted a proper feast. Macaroni and cheese, sweet potato casserole, corn pudding, green bean casserole, and an apple pie. My friends from Quebec would be bringing the meat, chicken from KFC, as nobody had access to turkey. They simply didn't have turkey meat in China, at least none that we could get living in a smaller city. Perhaps the high-end malls in Beijing had a supply, but that would be one helluva 16-hour train ride just for meat. The day prior, I had ventured out to the newest shopping plaza in the city center to visit the foreign goods store. They had the cheese, pasta, butter, brown sugar, and cream of mushroom soup that I would need, as well as paper plates and plastic forks. I spent the equivalent of $75 USD on these items alone. I purchased the apples, green beans, and corn from the wet market vendors downstairs. The vendors set up every day in the middle of the apartment complex, which provided easy access to fresh fruits and vegetables. All I needed now was the sweet potatoes.

About five blocks from my apartment, near a hairdresser in an alley, sat an old man with a large metal barrel in a cart. This was the roasted sweet potato vendor, and he was there every day in the winter. His barrel had a special compartment for coal, which he loaded on the bottom before placing the sweet potatoes on top of a protective metal grate. He roasted them for hours, still in the skins, and sold them as a tasty treat. School children especially loved the roasted sweet potatoes, and he routinely sold out after school was dismissed. Since they were already roasted, the sweet potatoes would be easy to mash into a casserole, and most of the hard work would be done for me.

Back at my apartment, it was a mad rush to assemble everything. I had purchased a small counter-top oven a few months prior, but it could only hold one dish at a time. I'd ordered my aluminum casserole dishes special from the Internet, and they barely fit in the oven. I decided to make the macaroni and cheese on the stovetop. But that still left the corn pudding, green bean casserole, and apple pie left for full cooking, and the sweet potato casserole needed at least fifteen minutes. I was looking at roughly four hours of cooking time, and realized that all of my food was going to have a nice gradient of temperatures. I decided the apple pie should be baked first, since nobody would balk at a room-temperature pie, then the corn pudding, then the green bean casserole. As soon as the green bean casserole was done, I would start the macaroni and cheese, and while that was cooking, I would warm up the sweet potato casserole, too. I spent the entire day in the kitchen.

Guests began arriving promptly at 5:00pm, and with them came more food. The much-needed KFC, mashed potatoes, freshly baked dinner rolls, plenty of beer and wine, and somehow someone had managed to make a pumpkin pie. I had ten friends in my apartment by then, and everyone had found a seat. I was busying myself with a group in the kitchen when I heard the next round of knocks on my apartment door. The English teachers had started arriving now, and were followed shortly by my university friends. The knocks on my apartment door became so frequent that I told my guests to just open the door for whoever knocked, no need to wait for me to open. Twenty people crowded into my apartment now, more than I'd planned for, and the kitchen was packed with food.

Two more people had brought KFC. Another knock on the door came. And another. And another. Word about my party had gotten out, it seemed, and everyone wanted a piece of metaphorical Thanksgiving pie, and the real apple pie was devoured. One friend came with a broken leg. We found a proper chair for her to sit on in the living room. My guests loved the idea of sitting on the blankets on the floor, and the cats were happy to have the attention, too. Another knock on the door. This time, someone had brought pizza! This was a relief since food was running low. By the end of the first ninety minutes, I counted thirty people in my apartment. Thirty! We were crowded elbow to elbow, but everyone was talking and laughing, mingling from one room to the other, helping themselves to drinks and food and cats. We kept the door to the smoking room closed, but eight people had camped permanently inside with others still coming and going.

I worried a bit about the noise, but it was well before bedtime, and decided to push the issue to the back of my mind. I was more concerned about keeping up with the trash and making sure I visited with everyone at least once. My apartment was full of people from across the globe – America, Canada, China, Venezuela, Japan, Korea, Brazil, Germany, the United Kingdom, Ireland, Finland, France, Spain, Pakistan, Bahrain, Guyana, Suriname, Kenya, Kazakhstan, Saudi Arabia, South Africa, Ghana, Belarus, Russia, and the Philippines. Perhaps a few other countries, too. The expat community in Jinan was a true melting pot. We even had our own version of English, with our own slang and cadence to accommodate all levels and origins of speakers.

Periodically, guests would leave the apartment to make a beer run down the street, returning with cases of room-temperature Qingdao, bottles of Changyu wine, the Chinese version of brandy, an armful of soju, and even two bottles of baijiu. Thanksgiving 2014 had turned into the biggest foreign party to date, and we were determined to live it up. At one point, however, I had to rescue Midas from a Canadian who tried to feed him beer. The cat disappeared into the sunroom after that, hiding in my laundry pile. Phoebe sauntered happily around the living room, roaming from one lap to the other while guests cooed in her direction.

Around 8:00pm, someone grabbed my arm. "Anna!" they panted, "Anna, the police are outside!" The police? Oh no, this couldn't be good. But only a few people in the apartment could speak Chinese well enough to communicate with the police. My British friend, Matt, volunteered to go downstairs and meet them with me. The others who could speak Chinese recoiled at the thought of the interaction, but I couldn't blame them for that. I went downstairs and outside with Matt. The police were waiting at the sheet-metal gates in front of the building.

"Do you live here?" an officer asked me as I approached.

"Yes, I do," I replied.

"Well, what are you doing in there?! We've had three calls tonight about the noise," the officer said.

"We're having a party," I tried to explain, but I didn't know the Chinese word for "Thanksgiving".

Luckily, Matt jumped in. "It's the Thanksgiving holiday for Americans today," he explained, "and so she invited some friends over to celebrate."

"How do you celebrate? With a big party?" asked a second officer, standing slightly behind the first.

"Usually, family gathers together, and we eat turkey," I explained.

"You have turkey in there?" the second officer asked.

"No," I said, "China doesn't have turkey. We ate KFC instead."

The officer huffed.

"How many people are in your house?" asked the first officer.

"About… 30, I think?" I responded.

"Yeah, between 28 and 33," Matt confirmed.

"So, you have 30 foreigners in your apartment?" the second officer asked.

"Yes," I said.

The officers stared at us in silence. We stared back, unmoving. The officers had the right to demand passports and visa information from any foreigner at any time for any reason, but not all the foreigners here tonight were following the laws of the country. Many of us, including myself, were working illegally while also attending university. Others were "technically" on internship visas.

"I'm really sorry about the noise," Matt told the officers.

"We'll tell everybody that they need to be quiet. We really didn't mean to inconvenience anybody." The officers seemed to like Matt.

"Well, it's almost 8:30pm on a Thursday night. Children are trying to sleep, you know. They have school tomorrow. And you're disturbing the old grannies that live here," the first officer said.

"You have until 10:00pm," the second officer said next. "Make sure everyone is gone by then. If we have to come back after that, we'll arrest whoever is inside."

"Yes, we understand, thank you, we'll make sure we're gone by then, thank you," Matt and I told the officers. We *were* making an awful racket, especially for a weekday, and the officers were walking away without even going inside. We considered ourselves very lucky, and bounded back up the three flights of stairs to tell everyone to get ready to leave.

After we relayed our encounter with the police to the group, two-thirds of the guests were gone by 9:00pm. The remaining third consisted of my core friends' group, and we all had the next day off work.

"To the clubs!" screamed an English teacher from South Carolina. "Tonight we turn up!" This girl partied with a ferocity that nobody else could match, and she expected us all to try and keep up with her. And so, we spent the rest of the night hopping from one club to the next until we decided to end the night at our favorite bar. The owner, who'd grown to be a close friend, gifted us a bottle of whiskey in celebration of the holiday.

"Party of the year was at your house, friend," Matt said, leaning into me close. "I don't think I'll ever forget it."

A Taste of Failure

Late into the spring semester at Shandong University, the French Canadians showed up on campus. There to learn the language and participate in cultural enrichment programs like learning Kung Fu, our summer school classmates soon found their footing around the international dorms. The university had several of these short-term programs available for foreign students. A handful of them would stay past their summer course, joining us for full-time classes in the fall. Jozie was among those who stayed.

Jozie's English wasn't perfect. Growing up in Quebec, French was her native language, leaving her with a thick accent. Her Chinese was almost as good as her English, however, and it felt like she breezed through whatever the language professors threw her way. She'd been in China before, living in the northern provinces for years, braving the cold winters and reveling in the gruff way the northerners went about their business. But she was thriving in Jinan, and we became fast friends.

Jozie was still presenting as male at this time; she wouldn't transition until after returning to Canada years later. In her mid-20s, Jozie's thick, wavy hair fell well past her shoulders. She dressed in all black, including her glasses, and was a fiend for metal music. But she also fell hard for all things kawaii, and relished the strange and weird fascinations that were constantly coming out of Japan. She was the type of girl you could find playing Mahjong with the old aunties by day and draining the bars of their baijiu by night. She was an atheist, despite her religious upbringing, and she was married to a Catholic woman, Gabby.

Gabby joined Jozie in Jinan a year later, taking up work as an English teacher while studying at the university. She was on a spousal visa, meaning she wasn't allowed to legally work or attend classes, but everybody always looked the other way. The university could feign ignorance and the school could bribe the police, so everybody won. Still, Gabby wasn't fond of the illegal avenues as she wasn't much of a rule breaker. She went along with it because that's just how things operated in China at the time, and everyone knew what questions not to ask.

While Jozie was fond of the underground death metal scene, Gabby was fond of cooking, and often brought her friends together for a meal. One early October, just days before the Mid-Autumn Festival, the celebration of the full moon nearest the autumn equinox, Gabby invited me over to help her and Jozie make mooncakes, a pastry with a thick, pasty filling and a smooth, chewy, golden exterior. Jozie had given me my first mooncake the year before, filled with lotus seed paste and the yolk of a salted duck egg. It was rich and delicious, sweet and savory, and despite its small size, much too weighty to be eaten in one sitting. I had no idea how to make them, however. They seemed much too complex for the average home baker, but Gabby was determined.

Jozie had purchased Gabby an oven shortly after moving into their apartment. She was one of the few foreigners who had such a luxury. We would certainly need it for the night. The mooncakes were shaped, as it turned out, by pressing the pastry into special intricately designed molds. Gabby was able to purchase these from TaoBao, the Chinese version of eBay. Then she and Jozie made a day of hopping from shop to shop around the city to pick up the other ingredients. Red beans, peanut oil, golden syrup, lye water, and salted duck eggs. The salted duck eggs she bought from a wet market vendor on the street near her apartment.

When Jozie answered the door that evening to let me in for the mooncake making, I could tell the air was tense. Things had already been going wrong. The red beans took hours to make into a proper paste, and the kitchen, which had already been cleaned twice that day, was a complete wreck. The lye water was lost. Flour was everywhere.

"Welcome to the mooncakes!" Jozie exclaimed, pushing the hair from her face. "Gabby is already started with the dough."

I smiled at the way she spoke English, slightly broken yet wholly understandable. Jozie handed me a warm beer as we headed back to the kitchen where Gabby was furiously kneading at the mooncake dough and cursing in French.

"I've already been cooking for five hours today!" she wailed when she saw me. "I've had enough!"

"Do you want me to take over? I can help," I offered.

"No!" she replied with determination. "I will *finish* this!"

I understood the feeling of wanting to finish what you started. Jozie moved to her laptop to play the latest BabyMetal song.

"You could help me wash dishes if you wanted," she suggested, shrugging.

I took her up on the offer. It wasn't that doing dishes excited me, but I felt awkward just standing around watching poor Gabby struggle while I did nothing but drink a beer. Providing her with a clean kitchen was the least that I could do. Jozie washed while I dried and put away, and by the time we were through, Gabby had the dough ready. I watched her through the window that divided the kitchen from the dining room as she slumped down into a kitchen chair and threw her head into her dough-laced hands.

"What's wrong?" I asked. "Was making the dough hard?"

"It's not just that," she responded, "it's everything! I've been planning this for over a month. I had to find the right molds on TaoBao, and had to get my Chinese coworker to buy it for me because it didn't want to take my passport number as my ID." In China, purchases made online are verified by your personal ID number, which is assigned upon birth. It acts as a sort of social security number, but used much more liberally.

Gabby continued, "And it took me hours to find the right eggs. You can find regular duck eggs anywhere, sure, and thousand-year-old duck eggs and marinated duck eggs and jellied duck eggs, but salted? I almost gave up! And the recipe…"

"Awh, *fuck* that recipe!" Jozie exclaimed as she sat down at the table with us. "You know how crazy the Chinese recipes are. Even I had some difficulties translating it, and it took us both to understand it."

"Yeah, like it said 'add sugar', but never said how much! Or what kind!" Gabby was starting to turn red. Chinese recipes are much less descriptive than Western recipes, often lacking exact measurements and cook times, taking a "cook with your heart" approach.

"But it's okay now, yeah? You did it," Jozie told Gabby, and soon we'll have delicious mooncakes and all your hard work will pay off."

"We're not done just yet," Gabby said. "We still have to peel the duck eggs. We'll need the whole dozen."

With that, Jozie stood up to retrieve the eggs, placing the bag – eggs come in a bag in China – gingerly on the table. We all reached in the bag to grab a couple, and began peeling the eggs. Immediately, a rotten stench hit my nose, causing me to squinch up my face.

"Are you guys sure these eggs are still good?" I asked. "They smell rotten to me."

"I don't know," said Jozie. "They do smell kinda bad, but maybe that's how they're supposed to be."

"I just bought them fresh!" Gabby cried. "They should be fine! They'll taste better in the mooncakes."

With the eggs peeled and the yolks placed in a bowl, Gabby took out what appeared to be a biscuit cutter from the kitchen.

"It came with the mooncake molds," she explained. "So we know how big the skins should be." Gabby began cutting out circles of dough while Jozie brought out the thick bean paste mixture for the filling.

"Okay, so now all we have to do is make a ball of filling around the egg yolks and then wrap it with the dough so it's all round," said Gabby, and the three of us set to work rolling the filling around our egg yolks. As the bean paste warmed under our palms, it began to melt and stick to our fingers. We knew we'd have to work quickly for this step.

I grabbed a circle of dough and placed my mooncake filling in the center. Gingerly, I folded the sides of the skin around the filling, folding from the left, then the right, then the top, then the… at just about the same time, all three of us discovered that the circles of dough we had were not, in fact, big enough to completely encase the mooncake filling.

I thought Gabby was going to cry. "Great, now we're going to have to reroll the dough and find a larger circle! I don't think

I have anything bigger! All I have are glasses and bowls!" she exclaimed.

"No, it's okay, it'll be alright, look!" said Jozie. "Just take some of this dough from another skin piece and put it over the space that's missing. Then you can pinch the pieces together. It looks a little weird but it will go in the mold anyway, right?"

Gabby wanted her mooncakes to be perfect, yet her kitchen adventuring was turning out to be anything but. She sighed in resignation, accepting that her mooncakes would have a bottom seam from our makeshift wrapping rather than being perfectly smooth and professional. We finished wrapping the skins in silence, Swedish metal music blaring from Jozie's laptop. We were deep in concentration, trying to stretch the dough over the filling without breaking it, aiming for an even thickness around the entire pastry, and wiping the bean paste from our hands. We ran out of duck eggs before we ran out of filling and dough, but we kept going. Not everybody enjoyed the duck eggs, anyway, and this way there would be enough left to share.

By the end of the hour, our fingers were cramped and the mooncakes were lined up in little balls across the table. We would tackle the molding next. The mold Gabby found online was a spring press device. The mooncake was placed on the table, the mooncake mold on top of it like a big stamp, and a firm push on the spring would send the mold down on top of the ball of dough and filling, pressing it into an ornate circle with a classic floral knot sculpted on the top. It was the easiest part of the process. At least in theory. The mooncakes were soft and warm from all the handling, and the dough stuck to the inside of the mold. We poked many mooncakes out with a chopstick, remade several completely, and jumped for joy when a mooncake came out of the mold without issue.

At last, we had a good twenty-five mooncakes to bake. The mooncakes required several egg washes. The first went on before the mooncakes went into the oven. Then another application after five minutes of baking. Then another after ten minutes. Then out of the oven to cool after fifteen. We had to bake in three batches due to the small size of the oven. As the first batch baked, a rather foul stench began to waft from the oven. It smelled like rotten eggs. We ignored it. The yolk-less mooncakes smelled much better while baking.

It was well past dark by the time the mooncakes were cooled enough to eat. The three of us tensed as we each bit into a salted duck egg mooncake.

I spit mine out immediately. The yolk was rotten! There was no mistaking it, with a sulfur smell that tinged the nose and a sour taste that was reminiscent of a trash can.

"Oh, it's terrible, Gabby!" I cried.

"No, it's fine!" she said, tears welling up in her eyes. "This is how they're supposed to taste!"

"I really do think it's rotten..." I said, then turned to Jozie. "What do you think?"

"I... uhm... well, it's not my favorite," she replied, not wanting to rock the boat. She would be the one dealing with the mooncake aftermath, after all.

I tried another bite. I tried so hard to chew and swallow, but instead I gagged. Gabby turned beet red. "I'm sorry! I'm so sorry! I just can't!" I said, turning to Gabby.

"It's fine," she huffed, not wanting to admit just how awful the mooncakes tasted. "We have plenty of mooncakes without the eggs, too."

Gabby needed space. And she needed us all out of her kitchen. Her experiment had failed, and it was going to take a minute for her to face that reckoning. A month of planning, a whole day of hard work in the kitchen, all to be foiled by spoiled duck eggs. She moved around the kitchen, grabbing a plastic to-go container and loading it up with a third of the non-duck-egg mooncakes. She was as ready for me to leave as I was ready to go.

"Thank you for helping," she told me, handing me the container of pastries.

"It was my pleasure," I smiled at her. "We'll have to do it again next year now that we know how to make them."

"Yes, next year we'll know everything!" said Jozie, a grin sweeping across her face. I hugged them both goodbye and set out on my walk home.

A block later, I tripped over a small pothole in the sidewalk. "No!" I cried out as I lost my grip on the mooncakes and their container flew out of my hands, scattering the cakes across the sidewalk and under the feet of the passers-by. I went down hard, landing on my hands and knees. The balls of my hands were busted, and so were each of my mooncakes. Not a single one had survived the fall. I never got a chance to try our plain cakes without the rotten duck eggs, and none of us were up for the task again the following year.

Lisa's Game

Lisa's Game, concocted by a 22-year-old Chinese medical student who learned her English from South Park, is a drinking card game that encompasses the spirit of truth or dare, meant to be played with at least four people and no more than eight. However, multiple decks can be combined to create variations of the game to accommodate more players.

To play Lisa's Game, you'll first need a deck of cards. Pull a whole suit from the deck, Ace through King. These will be your active cards. You may put the rest of the deck away.

Distribute the cards evenly until no cards are left. Some players may have more cards than others. This is intended and enhances the game. If more than seven people are playing, add an extra Two card to the active cards.

Each card has a designation, described as follows:

King – The King chooses the dare. The dare must be a specific activity, such as biting someone's ass.

Queen – The Queen chooses a number of times for the dare to be performed OR a duration of time for the dare to be performed. For example, bite someone's ass five times.

Jack – The Jack may choose to alter the number of times or duration of the dare by doubling the value, halving the value, or keeping the value the same. For example, bite someone's ass ten times.

Ace – The Ace chooses one card (or two, if two people are

involved in the dare) between the numbers Three and Ten. These cards must perform the dare. For example, the holder of the Ace may say, "card Three bites card Ten's ass."

Three through Ten – Cards Three through Ten are the hot cards. They do not make rules, but are subject to being picked by the Ace to perform the dare.

Two – The Two is a reverse card. If any card holder chosen to perform the dare is also holding a Two card, they may lay their Two on the table and the dare is reversed back to the Ace to perform.

If the chosen hot card does not want to perform the dare, they must finish their whole drink, no matter how much is left.

Got it? Now, let's see it in play.

"I've got the King! Let's see… I dare someone to bite another player's ass!"

"I've got the Queen. Let's say, bite them five times."

"I've got the Jack. We're doubling that to ten times!"

"Okay, I've got the Ace. I'm going to say that the three bites ten."

"Oh, I have the Three! But I also have the Two! So, *you'll* be doing the biting, Ace!"

And that's why I bit my friend Nathan's ass ten times.

Are We Part of a Scandal?

"Get over here, bitches!" Callie exclaimed from the sidewalk in front of the grocery store as our taxi rolled to a stop and four of us poured out of the car for a weekend adventure. Callie had lived in China for three years by the time she landed her live-in English teacher position for a family in Laiwu. One of the ten urban districts of Jinan, Laiwu sat about 50 miles southeast of Jinan with a considerably tiny population of 900,000 residents over 750 square miles. Callie had come to Jinan in 2012, taking up a teaching position at the Best Learning English training school where Katherine and I worked, and the three of us had become fast friends.

Callie was just as much of a social butterfly as I was, and it wasn't long before she was a staple of the Jinan expat community. She was well-loved among each of the teacher groups and university students alike, the older expats in Jinan for careers were impressed by her, and she made Chinese friends extremely easily. Her carrot-red hair and piercing blue eyes made her a spectacle for many of the locals, although she endured a fair number of japes about her curtains matching the drapes by a good deal of foreign men too.

Hailing from Iowa, Callie was a small-town girl with big dreams, and she was never in one spot for too long. By the time 2015 rolled around, she had worked as an English teacher at two training schools, a kindergarten, two universities, and had moved to the island province of Hainan before returning back to Shandong. She had also taken language classes with us at Shandong Normal University, and her Chinese was better than most. Although she was social, she was incredibly hard to get a hold of. Phone calls and text messages would go unanswered for days, and Callie had a bad habit of losing her phone. Since Laiwu was a ninety-minute drive from the Jinan city center, we were seeing less and less of her. So, when Callie invited a group of us to visit her for a weekend and scope out her town, we jumped at the opportunity.

Priscilla, JuJu, Ben, and I each stuffed a backpack into the trunk of a taxi on a brisk Monday morning. Since Saturdays and Sundays were the biggest days for private classes, teachers at training schools took their weekends on Monday and Tuesday. Sunday was our Friday. Monday was our Saturday. And so on. Ben was a mountain of a man, tall and broad, sporting thin glasses and a Geordie accent. He didn't care if he was joining a girl's weekend, he wanted an adventure! We were happy to oblige. JuJu, a former professional cheerleader from Utah, had become close friends with Callie since her arrival in Jinan earlier that year. She was one-quarter Chinese and was quickly picking up on the language. Juju was fit, smart, beautiful, and humble. Priscilla was considered a spectacle everywhere she went because she was Black. Although there were plenty of Black foreigners in our friends' groups, very few locals had ever seen a Black person. Priscilla was originally from Jamaica, although she'd moved to Florida as a teenager. She spoke with a thick Patois accent when she was angry or excited. And as for me, I was the fat one that spoke the best Chinese.

"*Hao jiu bu jian!* (Long time no see!)" we all cried to Callie as we clambered out of the taxi, hugging her tight. She had given us the address to the gate of a subdivision. Instead of the usual cluster of towering apartment complexes we saw two-story homes, an extreme rarity in China reserved for only the wealthiest of families. Owning an actual house, not just an apartment, full of modern amenities was the pinnacle of the Chinese Dream, and few would ever reach it. In front of the community stood a small grocery store, and Callie ushered us inside to collect a weekend's worth of snacks and beverages. Then, arms full of junk food, we were led to Callie's house.

The house itself was used as a second home for Callie's employers. Their main residence was on a strawberry farm on the outskirts of town, and on days when Callie wasn't teaching the children English, which was becoming increasingly more often, the family let her have the place all to herself. There were three bedrooms, two bathrooms, a living room, a sunroom, a dining room, and a kitchen, all with the most expensive furniture and appliances, ornately decorated antiques littering the house amidst toddler toys. Priscilla and I both claimed a bedroom. Juju would sleep with Callie in the king-sized master bed. Ben would take the couch. Taking it upon myself to place our drinks in the full-sized refrigerator, another rarity in China, I couldn't help but notice the pounds of cordyceps – an extremely expensive traditional Chinese medicine – crammed, unopened, in the back. Tens of thousands of yuan worth of cordyceps.

Callie approached me from behind. "I know," she said, peering into the refrigerator with me. "Isn't it insane? And check out what else there is!"

She moved over to a spot beside the sink and lifted up a bronze teapot unlike any teapot I'd ever seen before. The "pot" sat atop a tall stand, with six small spouts attached to the space where the pot and stand met. "I've only seen them use this once,"

Callie said, "and I have no clue what kind of tea it was."

"But," she continued, "I have a special treat for you all, come on!" She called us all into the living room, sat the teapot on the large wooden coffee table, and ran back to the kitchen to retrieve a package of tiny plastic cups. She placed a cup under each spout, and asked us to circle around.

"Three, two, one," she counted, and at the end of her countdown activated a special latch on the teapot that opened the spouts. A clear liquid came running out.

"It's baijiu!" Callie cried, and we clapped at both the teapot demonstration and the notion of drinking alcohol before noon. We took our shots then replaced our little cups under the spouts, despite baijiu—which is made from sorghum—tasting like paint thinner and having a very high alcohol content. Ben took two.

"Let's try it with Skittles," Callie said, and produced a package of the candy from a bag on the table. She dropped a skittle in each cup, then poured more baijiu into the teapot. We watched, mesmerized as it flowed out of all six spouts, filling each of the little cups. "If we wait a little bit, the flavor should soak in."

We cracked open a case of beer, passing around the warm bottles as we waited for our baijiu to eat away at the candy coating and give us a delicious treat. For the next fifteen minutes, Callie told us about her life in Laiwu. She had essentially become an au pair, with her Chinese family expecting her to watch after the kids when she wasn't teaching them English. She pushed back hard against that, though, especially since the youngest still wasn't potty trained. In China, babies and toddlers who are mobile, but not yet potty trained, do not wear diapers, but rather special pants with a large hole in the crotch so they can poop and pee at will. This leaves the caretakers with the responsibility of cleaning up the mess off the floor. Callie wasn't into cleaning up baby shit.

She also told us the history of the family, and how the father, Mr. Wen, came from old opium money. His family had gained wealth through poppy farming, although that had now changed to farming organic strawberries. The farming was suspiciously lucrative though, and Mr. Wen had connections with all the city officials, including the mayor. In fact, Mr. Wen would be giving us a tour of his strawberry farm later that day, and would be treating us to dinner that night.

Our stomachs collectively growled at the mention of food. It was well into lunchtime, and although we'd loaded up on snacks, what we really wanted was a meal. We threw our skittles baijiu shots back – nice and fruity – then headed out to Callie's favorite barbeque restaurant for goat kebabs and boiled peanuts. By then, it was warm enough for us to peel off our jackets and enjoy our meat and beer outside. When our bellies were full, it was time to meet Mr. Wen and his family for the strawberry farm tour.

Mr. Wen sent two drivers to pick us up from Callie's house, both handsome young men with fancy black BMWs, both of which belonged to Mr. Wen. One driver was introduced as a nephew, the other as a family friend. We first drove to Mr. Wen's countryside home, a sprawling single-story house with furniture that cost literally millions of yuan. Our jaws dropped as we entered the farmhouse and Mr. Wen called us over to him. Stepping around the puddles of his toddler's urine, we joined him for a photo on his six-person rosewood bench, ornate with hand-carved knots, floral patterns, and a dragon that spanned the entirety of the bench.

His wife was gruff, although she didn't mean to be. She loved her lavish lifestyle, and wanted desperately to make friends, but she had a resting bitch face and a sharp way of speaking that scared off most other women from even attempting to buddy up with her, or so Callie had said. When she heard me speak Chinese to Mr. Wen, she slid her arm under mine, grabbed my shoulder, and asked me to add her on WeChat so we could be friends. We exchanged contact information while Mr. Wen showed the rest of the group his collection of vases and art pieces.

Then, Mr. Wen got a phone call. He left us with his wife and children as he excused himself to another room, and Ben kneeled down to speak a bit of English to the oldest child, who was not quite five. The little girl, however, was too apprehensive of our foreign faces to be willing to play. When Mr. Wen returned, he informed us of some great news. The mayor would be joining us for dinner that night! Mr. Wen would be treating him and us as honored guests at the fanciest hotel restaurant in the city. He needed to take the time to prepare, but told us that shouldn't stop us from enjoying our farm tour. With that, he and another young man that appeared from the back room took off, leaving us with his wife, children, and the two drivers.

Eager to show us the farm, Mr. Wen's nephew directed us back into the cars, and we drove a short distance to a field of huge plastic greenhouses. Despite the weather still waning between snow one week and rain the next, the inside of the closest greenhouse was warm enough for us to roll up our sleeves. Large, lavish strawberries beckoned to be eaten straight from the vine. The fruit was as red as blood and so juicy they would gush when bitten into. The family didn't use any pesticides, the nephew bragged, and the fertilizer they used came directly from the neighboring farmers. We had our fill of berries as we toured the greenhouses, stopping to chat with the occasional worker and watching Juju and the nephew flirt. By the time we were done, evening had started to creep in behind the clouds and the shadows across the farm began to grow longer.

Juju sat in the front seat of the car as Mr. Wen's nephew drove us to the hotel restaurant. Callie followed behind in the car with Mr. Wen's wife and children. The hotel staff immediately ushered us to the top floor upon arrival, leading us to the largest dining room available. There was seating for twenty between two large round tables, and the room was complete with its own bathroom. We waited to be seated. We knew that the center seat, the highest seat of honor facing the door, would be reserved for either the mayor himself or Mr. Wen. To the right and left would be Mr. Wen's closest friends and honored guests. And while we were indeed those same honored guests, we didn't want to make any assumptions about seating, and milled about in the room until we were all herded to a table and told to sit. The waitresses brought in piping hot pots of green tea, and Mr. Wen's wife began ceremoniously filling our ceramic tea glasses.

"My husband will be here soon," she told me. "He's just getting some wine and waiting for the mayor to arrive." We smiled at each other and sipped our tea. I looked across the table to find Ben fidgeting in his seat. He was sweating bullets.

"What's wrong with you, Ben?" Priscilla asked.

"I've got to use the bathroom... bad," he responded. We weren't sure just *how* bad it was. Sometimes in China, the food poisonings would sneak up on you when you least expected it.

"Just go!" she said. "You can't hold it in forever!"

"You're right," Ben admitted, breathing in sharply. He stood up quickly and tried to quietly make his way to the bathroom, slipping behind the new guests that had just arrived. They were introduced to us as friends of Mr. Wen, and were seated at honored positions at the second table.

We smoked as we waited, throwing our cigarette butts on

the tile ground as was customary, drank tea, and had casual conversation with the other people in the room, although the language barrier prevented any deep discussion. The children complained of being hungry. Ben was still in the bathroom. Mr. Wen was still gone.

Another twenty minutes passed before Ben came back. I watched two of the men who were standing by the bathroom smoking slowly scuttle away from the open door. I'm sure Ben was embarrassed, but similar situations had happened to all of us, several times. Not ten minutes later, Mr. Wen burst through the door, carrying a three-foot-tall bottle of expensive Chinese wine.

"The mayor says he's not coming," Mr. Wen said, "but that doesn't mean we can't have a good time, hey? I brought wine!" And with that, the servers were given permission to begin the feast. Mr. Wen sat at the center of our table, facing the door. He put Juju, Callie, and myself on his left and Ben and Priscilla on his right. His two drivers had now turned into his servers, and they made their way around the table filling the small two-ounce glasses with wine and beer.

"Drink!" Mr. Wen would call out as the men poured. And we would drink, downing our entire glass as properly taught. Then the glasses were refilled.

"Half!" called out Mr. Wen, and we drained half our glasses. "Again!"

When the food arrived, the dishes were placed on the giant lazy Susan in the middle of the table, and spun gingerly towards the seat of honor. The table overflowed with cold tofu skins, steamed bok choy and mushrooms, fish soup, sweet and sour pork, dumplings, rice, pickled vegetables, fried vegetables, steamed beef chunks on the bone, all served course after course without respite. I supposed this was one of the larger feasts I'd attended. Obligation said we had to try it all. Mr. Wen had been picking the most expensive dishes, no doubt to impress the men who we learned were city officials that had joined us at the other table. Looking around, I felt honored being treated like a special guest, when really I was just a party kid out for adventure and debauchery. It was important to make a good impression though, so I played the part as politely as possible. When it came to local customs, I was the most knowledgeable and experienced, which meant I had to set the example.

"*San kou!* (Three mouths!)" Mr. Wen called out, indicating that he wanted us all to drink a glass of baijiu in three mouthfuls. We knew we had to grit our teeth and play along, lest we seem ungrateful. It was easy to shoot it all in one go, opening the throat and throwing it back. It was another thing entirely to space it out into three mouthfuls and try to savor it. Our glasses were refilled as soon as they were emptied.

There were fifteen of us total, between foreigners, family, and friends of the family that had come as honored guests for the mayor. A man from the other table approached me, handing me a cigarette. I gladly accepted, spewed out a round of *xie xie's* (thank you's), and held out my glass to cheers him. He attempted to tap his glass lower than mine. This was a common way of showing respect for someone in China, as the person of honor should have the highest glass. You should always try to clink the rim of your glass to the middle or bottom of the opposite person's glass. Since everyone wanted to be seen as the most respectful, and everyone wanted to exalt their friends, it became a game to see who could cheers the lowest, and friends would often find themselves lowering their glasses to the floor to get that lowest "clink". Mr. Wen never tried to go lower, though.

I held out my lighter to the man who had given me a cigarette. It would have been rude to refuse to smoke, since I was a smoker. In China, smokers shared their cigarettes during gatherings, often with the host insisting that the guest share a more expensive pack. In turn, the one receiving a cigarette would light the cigarettes for the other person. The man lightly tapped my fingers to indicate he was done with my flame, then he returned to his table.

Mr. Wen lit up a cigarette too, handing one to Ben. Eating and smoking went hand in hand in China, and people would stop eating mid-meal to enjoy a cigarette before returning to their feast. In the same vein, mealtime was also the time to consume alcohol in large quantities, although it was a little at a time spread out over the whole night. Still, those little shots here and there would certainly add up, and if you weren't careful, you could find yourself drunk on a lunch meeting with your boss.

Midway through the meal, Mr. Wen received a series of text messages informing him that the mayor was actually at the same hotel having dinner with a different group of men. He'd completely blown off Mr. Wen, and had shown him a great dishonor by not even popping in to say hello. Mr. Wen stewed in his seat. Then the waitresses arrived with bowls of the most expensive dish of the night, and my heart dropped.

Sea cucumber. Selling at an easy 500 yuan (or about $70 USD) per unit, sea cucumber was all the rage in the delicacy world. The demand for sea cucumber in China was high, as eating the marine animal is believed to have healing properties for an array of ailments ranging from impotence to cancer. It smelled like seaweed and wet dog, and it jiggled in its dish. I looked around the table and locked eyes with my foreign friends. We all had similar looks on our faces, a resignation to the fact that we'd have to eat the whole damn thing, even if we hated it. Mr. Wen had spent literally thousands on these critters.

I filled my glass with tea and carefully balanced the sea cucumber on my soup spoon before taking a bite. It was thick, slimy, and crunchy, like biting into a pig's ear that an old dog had been gnawing on. Like cartilage that had been soaked in sea water. And it was cold. My eyes widened as the taste and texture betrayed my tongue and churned my stomach, but I grabbed my tea and slammed the drink down my throat, washing the sea cucumber down with it. The taste wasn't terrible. It was bad, but it wasn't terrible. The texture, however, I just couldn't stand. I had enough trouble eating around bones and veins and faces without feeling ill – I grew up in a vegetarian household, and although I enjoyed eating meat, I wasn't used to the non-meaty parts of meat, especially fat and cartilage. This was like eating a nose.

I looked up and saw Ben wolfing his sea cucumber down in one go. That was certainly one way of doing it, getting it all out of the way at once. He squeezed his face together as he washed it down with a glass of baijiu. He wretched privately, but held his composure. I decided to follow his lead and go with big chunks followed by a beverage of choice. I didn't think I could stomach the baijiu, but luckily the table held a few bottles of juice. It was a selfish move, but I claimed one for myself. After filling up my cup, I stabbed my sea cucumber with my chopsticks. "Three big bites, Anna," I told myself, holding my chopsticks in one hand and my drink in the other. As soon as I took another bite, I was ready to open my throat and deposit the juice, letting it wash the sea cucumber down whole. A gag rose up from deep inside me, but I pushed it back down. And then again. And then a shot of baijiu. And then one last time. And then the thing was done.

Mr. Wen ate his sea cucumber with a pensive look on his face. He ate slowly, finishing after us, and he pushed back his chair to rise when he was finished. "All the foreigners come with me," he said, and so we all stood up and followed him as he exited the room. We could hear laughter coming from down the hallway as we walked towards the only other occupied room in the restaurant.

"Mr. Mayor!" Mr. Wen exclaimed as he reached the doorway of the room down the hall. "These are my foreigners. I wanted to introduce them to you." He walked into the room.

Inside the room were eight men, each dressed in fine business attire, baijiu bottles cluttering the table and cigarette butts littered across the ground. They all stood up as we entered and followed Mr. Wen single file through the room. We went around the entire table, each of us shaking hands with each of the businessmen and uttering a little *"ni hao"* (hello) with each new face. The mayor's face was beet red. He shook our hands and smiled at us, but glared at Mr. Wen. We all stayed silent, let him parade us around, and quickened our pace to return to our own room back down the hall. The whole ordeal seemed to make Mr. Wen feel better though. A smile had reappeared on his face, wider than it had ever been before.

We ate for longer still, dish after dish joining the lazy Susan. When our baijiu ran out, Mr. Wen sent his nephew out for whiskey, returning with a bottle of Jack Daniels. It was well past dark by the time the rice, the last dish to be served, was brought to the table. And we were all well past drunk, save for Mr. Wen's wife and children. Mr. Wen wasn't done with our party after dinner was over, however, and while he said goodbye to most of his guests and sent his wife and kids home, he directed three young men (including his nephew) and all the foreigners to come with him to KTV, a popular karaoke box establishment. It was impossible to skip karaoke in China, and we loved making fools of ourselves while belting out 90s pop hits. We were down.

Standing outside the hotel, Mr. Wen's drivers pulled up next to us, except one BMW had now been replaced with a sleek, white Tesla. Juju purred at the sight. Ben's jaw dropped. It was the newest Model X, equipped with every imaginable bell and whistle. We took turns sitting inside as Mr. Wen showed us all the cool features. "Please let me ride in this Tesla," Juju said, grinning ear to ear. Of course, nobody else minded. Mr. Wen and Callie took the front seats. His nephew and Juju took the back. The rest of us followed behind in the BMW.

The KTV room Mr. Wen booked wasn't the biggest or the most lavish, but it came with plenty of beer, pumpkin seeds, and China's favorite party drink – whiskey and black tea with lemon, mixed together in a large pitcher, available at every club. We were lucky and got it over ice. As we filed into our karaoke room, Mr. Liu positioned himself on the cushioned bench directly in front of the large television screen. His men sat beside him. Ben and Callie were down on the dance floor, queuing songs into the playlist and taking requests from Mr. Wen. Looking around, I noticed that his nephew and Juju were nowhere in sight. Where'd they go?

I didn't have too much time to think about it though, as a microphone was soon shoved into my face. "Anna, sing this one, the one about the lonely lady on her couch!" Ben exclaimed, "you sing it so well! I bet it'll really impress them." He was right, I was pretty good at this song and truly enjoyed singing it. We swapped places so I was closer to the television. Midway through the song, I saw Juju silently slip inside the room. Mr. Wen's nephew followed a few moments later. When the song was over, we handed the microphone over to our Chinese friends and huddled around Juju.

"So…" Priscilla started, "where ya been?"

Juju blushed, then laughed. "Okay fine," she blurted out, "we fucked in the Tesla! And it was great." We gave her a round of cheers then handed her a glass of the whiskey and tea cocktail. Mr. Wen's nephew grabbed the microphone to sing the next song, avoiding eye contact with everyone but smiling all the same.

As the singing, drinking, and smoking progressed, I found myself seated next to Mr. Wen as he cracked open pumpkin seeds with his teeth, spitting the shells on the ground. We had gotten onto the topic of infidelity in Chinese marriages.

"I really do love my wife," Mr. Wen said, seed in his teeth, "but I'm not good to her in this aspect. I sleep around a lot."

"Would you be okay if it were her sleeping around behind your back?" I asked him not unkindly. This was a sore spot for me, as I'd been in multiple relationships with Chinese men that either resulted in them cheating or me finding out I was the side piece. Still, I knew that arguing about it wouldn't help get through to anyone. I'd have to be gentle. And logical.

"That would tear me up!" he responded. "I can't bear to think about her with someone else!"

"I'm sure she feels the same as you," I suggested, and handed Mr. Wen a cigarette.

"Gah, but I get so angry with her!" he exclaimed, throwing his hands in the air. "She just doesn't listen to me, she always wants more and more from me!"

"Think about all she gives you, Mr. Wen," I said. "She's given you children and raises them every day, she keeps your house tidy and cooks for you. She helps with the farm and is by your side.

And she loves you, right? And you love her?"

"Yes, we still love each other very much," he said, taking a long drag from his smoke.

I moved from a sitting position on the bench down to one knee on the floor. "Then I'm begging you, Mr. Wen, look, I'm physically begging you, stop cheating on your wife. You know it's wrong. You're a good man inside, I know it, so please, be a good example. Think of your children!"

Suddenly, tears welled up in Mr. Wen's eyes. "You're right," he said, "I can be good! I can! Thank you." He reached a hand down to help me up off the ground, wiping his eyes with the other.

As Callie and Ben dueted a Britney Spears song, I noticed we were missing Priscilla. I remembered watching her leave, and had assumed she went in search of the restroom. But it had been a while now… where could she be? Did she fall in?

I went searching for her, and found her outside, sitting on the steps in front of the KTV, struggling to breathe. Priscilla had asthma, and the combination of a night's worth of smoking plus late spring allergies had given her an episode. But she'd left her inhaler behind at the house, and now she was coughing hard.

"Please," she managed between coughing fits, "I need water!"

Ben had followed me outside, and upon seeing Priscilla's state, ran back inside to retrieve the water. He came rushing back out a moment later.

"Here, I got water!" he shouted, holding out the bottle to Priscilla. But the KTV waitresses and Mr. Wen's nephew came running up behind him.

"It's not water! It's not water!" they collectively cried. Mr. Wen's nephew grabbed the water bottle Ben had brought, thrusting a new one into my hands. "Tell her she can have this, this one is okay to drink," he said.

Priscilla drank like her life depended on it. We didn't dare ask what was in the other bottle, although we later speculated it may have been laced with fresh organic strawberries from the farm. By the time Priscilla had finished her water, her coughing was under control, but we needed to get her home. The time in our karaoke room had almost expired, so it was a good time to end the night. This time, Priscilla, Ben and I rode in the Tesla.

Midnight was approaching by the time we arrived back at the house in the gated subdivision. Our Chinese companions were ready to go home and go to bed, but for us, being the professional partiers that we were, the night was still somewhat young. We didn't have anywhere to go, per se, but we found each other entertaining enough to keep the night alive.

"Juju, I gotta say, I'm jealous you got laid," I laughed as I sat on the living room floor, sipping skittles-laced baijiu.

"The night is young!" she replied. "And there are plenty of men in this city." She flashed me a wink.

Hookup culture in China was just starting to blossom, with special "dating" apps and secret QQ chat rooms made just for "casual conversation" in your local city. Being children of the times, we knew all about these casual conversations and how to access them. I pulled out my phone and opened my QQ app, setting my location to Laiwu and searching for "Laiwu Night Chat" (chat being a euphemism for sex in Chinese) and found a room with a little over 100 active users.

"Tell them you're a foreigner!" Ben urged. "That'll get you some!"

In truth, being a foreigner gave me an edge when it came to casual sex. I was viewed as something exotic, like a forbidden fruit that everyone wanted to taste, although my weight was a big turn off. As soon as I mentioned that I was an expat to the chat room, a dozen private messages flooded my app. I shared with the group, weeding out those who just wanted pictures and guys who were all talk and no action. Until finally, someone seemed promising. He was close by, would pick me up, and pay for the hotel. What a perfect gentleman. We arranged to meet at the gates of the subdivision, and Priscilla and Juju escorted me outside to wait.

My hookup and I had moved from QQ to text, so I shared his phone number and QQ information with my friends. In case anything happened, at least they'd have that to go off of. In hookup culture, especially in China, we didn't think much about the potential for danger. Rather, we just trusted that we would be inherently okay.

A taxi pulled up in front of the gate house, and a man stepped out. He told me he was 25, but he looked more like 20. To be honest, I had difficulty telling the ages of most Chinese people. It felt like they stayed younger for longer, as opposed to white Westerners who often appeared older than their true age. He stood beside the open taxi door and smiled at me.

"*Ni hao, mei nü* (hello, beautiful lady)," he said to me, "it's a beautiful night, isn't it?"

"If you hurt her, we'll hurt you!" Juju told him, only half joking.

He smiled at her and laughed nervously. "I'm not a bad guy or anything," he told Juju.

My hookup helped me into the back seat of the taxi, then sat himself in the front passenger seat. I was a bit disappointed by his choice, as I was hoping for a bit of a make-out session on the way to the hotel, but as he passed cigarettes to both me and the taxi driver, I could tell he was just trying to be respectful. And he looked nervous. All of the alcohol in my system made sure I wasn't the least bit nervous.

The hotel we arrived at looked pretty cheap and sleazy. It wasn't a chain hotel, but rather a mom-and-pop joint. I didn't care too much, since we didn't need to stay there for very long. He registered for a room and we proceeded up the stairs, unlocking the door with a small metal key attached to a tab. We could barely wait for the door to close before we started undressing. I was quicker than he was, and found myself completely naked on the bed while he was still standing with his pants on.

"Wait, wait just a second," he said, then shifted his pants and walked out of the room. When he came back in the room, another man followed behind him. It all happened so fast. They walked in. They both looked at me. I looked at them. We looked at each other. The tension was palpable. And then? They ran. One of them fully clothed and the other half naked, turned around and bolted out of the room as quickly as they'd entered, footsteps thundering down the hall as they ran.

I was utterly bewildered. What the hell was *that*? That had certainly never happened before. Were they planning something nefarious, only to be scared off? Was it all a big joke? This wasn't the first time more than one guy had tagged along on a solo adventure… that was a common tactic at the time, for one friend to suddenly become two, so I wasn't completely startled or surprised by the second man's presence. But that was certainly the first time someone had ever looked at my naked body and then literally ran away. I felt a little angry, actually. All I wanted was sex, and now I was left with, what, tomfoolery?

I dressed quickly and pulled out my phone only to realize it was dead. Which was perfect, because I didn't have the address back to Callie's house memorized. As I walked out of the hotel to find a taxi, I looked down the alleyway towards the road only to find my hookup, his friend, and another young man standing in a circle talking. I began to walk towards them, since that was the only direction I could go, but once my hookup saw me, he let out a shrill squeak, grabbed his friend, and the two of them began running again, the third friend quickly following suit.

I don't know what came over me then except a wave of rage. Whether it was misplaced or not, I couldn't tell, but I felt like I was being treated as less-than-human, and I didn't like it. So, I chased them. It must have been quite the spectacle, watching an overweight white woman run after three skinny men, one of them shirtless. I chased them for a block before they split off into two directions. I was panting hard, but the alcohol fueled my adrenaline, and I wanted answers. As my hookup and the third friend split off to the left, the second friend, who was the first one to start running, veered off to the right. I followed on his heels, ignoring the traffic lights as I crossed the intersection.

He stumbled on the uneven sidewalk, and went down hard. I took the opportunity to break into a sprint and close the gap between us. I reached him just as he was standing up, and just before he could run again, I reached out and grabbed a hold of his big, puffy black jacket.

"Let me go!" he screamed, trying to pull his coat from my grasp.

"No! What the fuck are you doing?!" I cried out. "Why did you look at me and run?!"

The man unzipped his coat and slipped out of it, leaving me holding onto just the clothing with no man inside. He bounced away from me.

"I'm only sixteen!" he cried. "I just wanted to see a naked foreigner!"

"SIXTEEN?!" I shouted in both shock and anger. Looking at him up close for the first time, I could see that he was clearly a teenager, and although the age of consent in China is fourteen, I had no interest in having sex with what I still considered to be a child. I immediately wondered how old my hookup had been. He certainly didn't look like a teenager, and he said he was twenty-five, but maybe he was lying? Maybe I hadn't noticed because I was so drunk? In either case, I was fuming.

"You're sixteen years old and tried to have sex with a twenty-four-year-old?" I shouted at him. "That's terrible! You shouldn't be doing that!" I took a step closer to him and waved his jacket at him in a scolding manner. "You need to be in bed! Not tricking women to see them naked! Do you know what kinds of trouble you could have gotten yourself into? And me, too!"

The boy didn't wait for me to say more, but rather turned on his heels and flew down the sidewalk, forgetting his coat. I didn't follow this time, but rather watched him run as fast as he could into the night. A taxi crept up beside me as I stood there, smoke rolling from the windows as the driver puffed on a cigarette.

"What did he do?" the driver asked, chuckling.

"He… I…" I started, but wasn't sure how to continue.

"I saw the whole thing," the driver said, "from the hotel all the way down here. I couldn't help but follow. I wanted to see how it would end." He coughed as he chuckled again.

"I was going to have sex with his friend… but they… they ran away! And then he told me he's only sixteen! SIXTEEN!" I cried. "I almost hooked up with a baby!"

"And now you have his jacket," the taxi driver smiled. "What are you going to do with it?"

"I guess I'll keep it," I shrugged. "I can't find him to give it back."

The driver laughed, then paused to take another drag of his cigarette. "So, where are you going now?" he asked.

"I want to go home," I told him, "but my phone is dead, and I don't know the address, so I don't know what I'm going to do next, honestly."

"Hop in," he said. "I'll get you there."

I took him up on his offer for a ride, and on his offer for a cigarette. Without the address, all I could do was describe the subdivision. He seemed to know where I was talking about right away, and he sang to himself as he drove me back.

"Don't worry about paying me," he said when we arrived, the first glimpses of light filtering through the sky. "Watching that whole thing was payment enough!"

I thanked him profusely and waved as he drove away.

I didn't know exactly what time it was, but the first stretches of daylight had already begun to appear in the sky. That meant it was at least 5:00am – Shandong got bright early. I navigated my way around the community gatehouse and found Callie's house again. I expected to need to pound on the door for a good minute in order to wake somebody up to let me in, but to my surprise, Priscilla flung the door open after only the first round of banging.

"There you are!" she exclaimed. "We've been waiting for you!"

"Have you really been waiting up all night for me?" I asked, feeling my eyes start to hurt from being so tired.

"Well, it was half and half," she said. "We got caught up in ourselves just talking the night away, but we were worried about you, too. You were supposed to come home right away! How long did you all take, you saucy wench!"

"Oh boy, do I have a story for you," I began, searching the

house for an unopened bottle of water to quench my growing thirst.

I followed Priscilla into the master bedroom where Callie and Juju were tangled up in sheets and blankets, sprawled all over the bed, giggling to each other.

"Anna!" they both called out in unison. Ben had been asleep on the living room couch, but the commotion of me returning home had woken him up, and he stumbled into the room behind us.

I told them all what had happened that night after I left, leaving out no details. They almost didn't believe me, until I held up the jacket I still had with me. Then they all burst out laughing.

"That poor kid!' Juju cried. "He must have been terrified! Here's this foreigner chasing him down the street all alone at night, the boy just wanted to see some pussy!"

Ben looked a little worried. "Couldn't you get in trouble, you know, for almost having sex with minors or something?"

"The age of consent in China is fourteen," Callie chimed in, "so she won't get in trouble for that. But she might get in trouble for stealing a jacket!" She cackled with laughter.

I turned to Ben. "Right now, I'm just happy that *almost* having sex isn't the same as *actually* having sex. I don't know how old the guy was who picked me up, but at this point, I don't think I want to know!"

In truth, I was feeling a little sick to my stomach, but I wasn't sure if it stemmed from the fact that I'd been drinking all night or from the fact that I'd almost fornicated with a teenager. Either way, I was ready to lay down and go to sleep. We all decided sleep was in our collective best interest. It was just now broaching on 6:00am, and if we slept until noon, we'd have plenty of time to make it back before dinnertime. But exactly two hours later, we

Unedited Author's Proof

were all roused from our sleep by a series of loud bangs.

BANG! BANG! BANG!

What was that?

Again. BANG! BANG! BANG!

We realized it was someone pounding on the front door. By the time I crawled out of bed and made my way to the front of the house, Callie and Ben were awake and heading in the same direction. We let Callie open the door, and on the porch stood a group of four police officers. Everyone turned and looked at me. I felt my face flush and my knees tremble a bit. I knew I was going to get arrested for sure, and I even had the evidence – the jacket – right out in the open on the dining room table.

The police pushed their way inside the doorway, but only one officer spoke.

"What are you all doing here?" she asked.

"I live here," Callie said, her Chinese wavering as she groped for the right words through the haze of sleep that still lingered on her brain, "and these are my friends. They're visiting from Jinan."

"You're supposed to register at the police station every time you spend the night somewhere other than where your visa is registered," the officer stated gruffly. "Show me your passports!"

Priscilla rushed to wake Juju and told her what was going on. We scurried around the house trying to find our wallets and purses. One by one, we handed over our passports. The officer thumbed through each of them.

"You've been in China for this long," she said while staring at one of the American passports, "you know the rules. You didn't register. You're all breaking the law right now."

We honestly didn't think it was going to be that big of a deal. We knew about needing to register, but it was only going to be for one night, and it was a rule that almost nobody followed,

Unedited Author's Proof
Unedited Author's Proof

anyway. Sure, we were all registered in Jinan, and regularly updated our registrations as needed, but for an overnight stay, I don't think it crossed anyone's mind.

Callie began to profusely apologize, but the officer put a hand up to silence her. They all looked intimidating in their black, pressed uniforms with pistols clipped to their belts. It wasn't every day you saw a gun in China. I wondered if the officer had ever needed to use hers before.

"You can stay since you're registered here," she said to Callie, "but everyone else has two hours to leave the city. Pack up and go, now. We'll be back to make sure they've actually left. Their time starts now." And with that, the three silent officers filed out of the door while the speaking officer handed us back our passports. She slammed the door as she left.

Where the others may have felt a sense of panic, I felt a sense of relief. They weren't here for me after all. Most likely, they were here because Mr. Wen had pissed off the mayor when he paraded us around his dinner affair the previous night, and this was his way of getting revenge. I pictured him stewing in his luxury five-bedroom home, mumbling to himself. "Were those foreigners even registered? No? Then get them the *fuck* out of my town!"

My limbs felt limp and my eyes ached as we all scurried about the house packing up. I desperately needed sleep and rest, and without it, I felt as though I was painfully melting into the floor. We skipped both breakfast and folding our clothes as we shoved our belongings back into our bags and tried to help Callie straighten up. It took us less than an hour—we knew the police were watching, and even though they could see us, we didn't want to see them again. Callie walked us out to the roadway and stood with us until we found a taxi willing to take us all the way back to Jinan. At 200 yuan, the price was a little steep, and we knew the driver was taking advantage of us, but we couldn't afford to argue. We split the fare four ways and clambered into the taxi.

The car stayed silent until we cleared the city limits. Then, Ben let out a chuckle. "Well, that was an adventure!" he said. We all burst out laughing, only to clutch our heads immediately after at the collective headache we all shared. Laying my head gingerly on the rear passenger window, I watched the land slowly change from vast farms back to the concrete jungle, and vowed never again to go to Laiwu.

It's Hard to Make Hamburgers

The fourth time I found myself in front of the police, I was holding a bag of meat. My roommate, Micah, stood in his house slippers as the snow drifted down around us. He slipped his hand inside his pocket, rummaging for one… two… three… four little candies. He pulled them out and held his hand out in my direction, palm open.

"Here," he said. "Pocket Skittles." I took two, chewing the yellow one immediately and sucking the red candy coating off the other.

We had been up all night drinking, and now the morning sun was high enough to illuminate the city through the clouds. Winters were long and harsh in Jinan, and Micah and I would warm our bodies by splitting bottles of sweet red wines and oaky brandies. Last night had been a "wine and tears" night, which was what we called our ritual of hashing through our traumas with one another, letting our emotions simply flow as we discussed the vile natures of those who have harmed us. I had more trauma to process than Micah, however, so the "tears" were more for me, and the "wine" was more for him.

The week had been long, and our stress had been building up to the point where, when we hit the nearest Uni-Mart, China's favorite convenience store chain, we grabbed not just one, but *three* bottles of wine. It was a week before payday, which meant we were nearing broke. As such, we had to settle for the cheapest wine available. Luckily, the cheapest bottle was also the biggest, holding 1.5 liters of a sickly sweet, deeply pink wine that we fondly referred to as "Kool-Aid". And at 13% alcohol content, it would always accomplish its purpose.

Since as teachers we worked weekends, Mondays became our Saturdays. This Saturday, we opted for each other's company instead of the usual bar scene. It wasn't that we were attracted to each other physically—Micah was asexual, and I had just left a relationship with a clinical psychopath—but we were certainly drawn to each other's wit. Occasionally, we just wanted the intimacy of friendship and the comfort of the apartment we shared. And we both loved to cook.

"Good Lord, I could go for a hamburger right now!" Micah had exclaimed around 2:00 am.

Hamburgers were expensive to buy in China, and most of them just didn't taste right. Sure, the McDonald's was a familiar taste, but fast food never quite hit the spot like a homemade meal, and prices were generally more expensive than the average restaurant.

"Have you ever had a butter burger?" I asked, taking a big gulp of wine and lighting up a cigarette.

"What's a butter burger?" Micah asked, full of curiosity.

"You basically just fry the patties in a skillet with a bunch of butter. Then sop up the juice with the bun, too," I explained. I could see Micha was salivating.

"Okay, we've gotta do this tomorrow, we're *definitely* going to make butter burgers!" Micah said assuredly.

"We're totally not," I laughed. "We're going to go to bed and wake up so hungover that all we can do is crawl to the couch. We're not going to want to get up and go to the store for all the ingredients."

"Yeah, you're right…" Micah reluctantly agreed.

"Unless…" I started.

"Unless?" Micah repeated.

"Unless we just stay up. The Muslim Quarter opens up at 5:00am," I suggested.

The Muslim Quarter was famous in Jinan for its barbeque. More specifically, its goat barbeque. Every night, the half-acre lot in front of the quarter would be filled with hungry tourists and locals alike. Beer was in high demand at the barbeque houses too, and although the workers wouldn't drink the beer themselves, they were happy to serve it to any paying customer. Behind the barbeque houses sat a row of shops. This was the only place in the city one could find halal meat, and the quality of meat available was much higher and less fatty than what could be found in the grocery stores. It wasn't any more expensive, either.

Micah's eyes widened. "The Muslim Quarter!" he said excitedly, then continued, "We'll take my motorbike."

And so it was decided we'd leave the house right at 5:00am to arrive at the quarter by 5:30am, which should give the shops plenty of time to open. The meat didn't have to be on display; we already knew which shop to visit for the best ground beef. The only thing left to do was to occupy ourselves for the remaining three hours until our departure time.

By the time we left our apartment, it had begun to snow. A solid half-inch of snow already covered the ground, left over from the previous week's snowstorm, preserved with the help of the increasingly brisk winter air. The city's winters were as blistering cold as the summers were sweltering hot. We'd heard another storm was on the move, but it wasn't supposed to arrive until the afternoon. Still, we decided to take my umbrella—an immense, black umbrella big enough for two people, the hilt of a broadsword replacing the handle, hence its name "sword-brella"—to keep our heads clear of any snow or sleet we might encounter on our way. I sat on the back of Micah's broad motorbike. It was a beast of a machine with a twenty-pound rechargeable battery that had to be hauled inside multiple times a week. I balanced precariously on the seat, reassuring myself that I wasn't afraid of falling off, and that I didn't need to grab onto Micah for dear life. Besides, I had to man the umbrella. I gripped the back of the motorbike with one hand, and held the umbrella above our heads with the other. Micah was still in his house slippers, but we were so drunk by this point, neither of us had the ability to care about winter footwear. The city streets would all be clear, anyway.

The wind hammered into us as we sped from the LiSha District to the downtown area. This proved problematic, as each gust would lift the umbrella suddenly, forcing me to hold on with both hands to keep it from flying away. Eventually, we had to stop so I could fold the umbrella down, but by then, the snow was coming down fast.

We reached the Muslim Quarter right on time – it was barely after 5:30 am, and the majority of shops were open and catering to customers. You didn't go inside these shops, but rather they served customers from counters at their shop fronts. We found the beef store. We bought two pounds of beef.

"Can you grind it for us, please?" I asked the store clerk, snow sticking to my hair.

"No," the clerk said, and turned her back to us. What an unexpected answer!

"Hang on," Micah said to her, thinking perhaps she'd mis-heard us since our Chinese wasn't perfect. "She asked you to grind the meat," he said, pointing to the meat grinder sitting on the desk behind the counter.

"No, I won't," the clerk repeated.

"Why not?" Micah questioned. "The meat grinder is right there! And we need it ground."

"I don't want to!" the store clerk snapped at us, then waved us away with a shooing motion.

"No!" I exclaimed drunkenly. "That's not fair! You ground the other people's meat! Why won't you grind ours?"

The clerk ignored us. Was it because we were foreigners? Not everybody was fond of foreigners in China, and they usually let us know. Could it be because we were totally trashed, drunkenly swaying in front of her shop with bloodshot eyes and alcohol on our breaths? Perhaps, but we'd been polite, and we were in good moods. It didn't make sense! I decided now would be a good time to argue.

"We told you we wanted ground beef when we bought the meat, so it has to be ground!" I yelled in frustration.

"We can't grind it up ourselves," Micah added angrily. There was a crowd growing around us now.

The clerk yelled back at us, "I don't have to if I don't want to!"

"Fine," I stated coldly, "but I'm not leaving here until you grind it up!" I would be damned if I didn't get a butter burger today.

I looked hesitantly at Micah, feeling a little unsure of myself. He looked confidently back at me, and stomped his foot, as if to say that he was staying right where he was. I took comfort in the solidarity, and found my bravery again. I stared hard at the clerk, and she stared hard back. Then the crowd began to part.

"Hey! What's going on here?" cried a police officer as he approached the shop counter. We both took a step back, turning to the officers.

I held up the bag of meat, and told them with a whine, "She won't grind our meat!"

"That's what this is all about?" questioned a second officer that had appeared beside him.

"YES!" Micah exclaimed. "It's JUST about the meat. All we want is ground meat."

The first officer pointed towards the awning of a closed shop. "Go wait over there," he commanded us. We obeyed. There, we were sheltered from the snow building up on the asphalt. I looked at Micah's feet as we stood under the awning, digging around in his pockets for candy. I wondered if he was as cold as he looked.

"We're in the right, right?" I asked him.

"Oh, we're totally in the right," he nodded deeply. Then he stumbled a little, alcohol still well alive in his system.

I wondered how the police had arrived on scene so quickly. But since we were downtown and the police were on foot, I thought maybe they were regularly stationed here this time of day. The early morning light brought the bustle of trucking-in the dozens of slaughtered goats needed for the daily barbeque, so the front of the quarter was absolutely packed with men and women hauling goats, cleaning tables, and prepping for the inevitable rush of customers that would start around lunchtime and last well past midnight. It would come as no surprise to know the police were there to supervise.

The first officer approached us. "Your passports," he said, holding out his hand.

Micah and I looked at each other. "We don't have them," I said.

"Why not?" questioned the officer, his eyes narrowing.

"You're supposed to have them at all times."

This was true. As foreigners, it was the law that our passports must be available on-person for inspection at any time. Yet, none of us followed this law. We all felt it was too dangerous to tote around our passports wherever we went, so we all left them at home unless we were traveling. I tried explaining this to the officer.

"They're at our apartments and –" I began, but was promptly cut off.

"Where are your apartments?" inquired the officer.

"They're at LiSha DaSha," Micah said, and told the officer the full address.

"And what are you doing here?" the officer asked. We both tensed. Micah was in China legally; he had a four-year degree and had come through a proper recruiter. I, on the other hand, was not working legally. My visa was an internship visa meant for a school I'd left a semester ago, which meant that if the police decided to do any real digging, my previous employer, my current employer, and myself would all need to grease a few palms. I held my breath.

"We're English teachers," Micah responded.

"No," sighed the officer, "what are you doing *here*, in the Muslim Quarter? This early in the morning?" I let go of my breath.

"Getting meat," we both responded, only slightly out of sync with one another.

"But *she* won't grind it," Micah continued, using his jaw to point to the clerk.

The second officer approached, expertly positioning himself to block our only path of escape should we choose to run.

"What are they doing here?" the second officer asked.

"Buying meat…" trailed the first officer.

"No, I meant what are they doing in China?" the second officer corrected. I tensed again.

"They're teachers," replied the first.

"At the same school?" asked the second.

"Not the same," Micah and I both said, again together, with better timing this round.

"And why are you causing trouble?" the second officer asked, turning to us.

"We weren't *trying* to cause trouble," I tried to explain. "We bought ground beef, but the clerk refuses to grind it!" I was wondering how many more times we'd have to explain this story today, and whether we'd be telling it to our friends or more officers.

"*Ai!*" we heard a new voice chime in from beside us, followed by a slow, "I'm coming, I'm coming."

A hunched old Hui woman approached us, swaying back and forth as she hobbled along.

"Give me the meat," she said. "I'll grind it, I'll grind it."

I handed her the bag of meat, spilling out a thousand thank-you's. The four of us watched as she hobbled back to her shop, the metal overhead rolling door only half-raised. She ducked under, and was gone from sight. Three moments later, she reappeared, hobbled back our way, and handed me the bag of freshly ground beef.

"Well, that settles it, then," the first officer spoke, breaking the silence.

"It's time for you to leave," said the second officer, motioning for us to be on our way. Were we really not going to get in trouble? I was starting to sober up a little, and was starting to feel a little ridiculous. Maybe we were in the wrong after all? Either way, I think the officers just wanted to get rid of us as quickly as possible, get out of everyone's hair and back to our own corner of the city.

We wasted no time leaving before the officers couldchange their minds. There was enough snow on the ground now to make the asphalt slick, and I wondered if Micah was alright in his slippers. The officers ushered us over to Micah's motorbike and watched as we both climbed on.

"These had better be the best damn burgers in the whole world," I thought to myself as Micah turned the key and propelled the bike forward.

As Micah turned his bike around the corner to put us back on the main road, we both heard a loud THWACK and pain shot through my body. He had taken the turn a little too wide, swinging a little too close to the metal barrier between the bike and car lanes. My knee, which was sticking out from the side of the bike as I perched on the back, had made direct impact with the first pole of the barrier.

Micah stopped the bike right away and helped pull me off.

"I don't think I can move it, Micah!" I cried. This was the first time I'd experienced both pain and numbness together. Sitting on the sidewalk, Micah braced his hand under my thigh as I tried to extend and retract my leg. My kneecap felt like it was on fire. A big, purple bruise was already starting to form, although the skin where the barrier had made impact was scraped white.

After a couple of big breaths and several minutes of increased movement, I decided that I didn't immediately need the hospital. Nothing was broken. I could still twist and bend, and even though it hurt, the pain wasn't excruciating anymore. I couldn't walk properly, though. Putting weight on my knee was too painful. I leaned heavily on Micah as he helped me back onto his motorbike. I had rolled up my pants to expose my knee on the street, but the swelling was so bad now that my pants wouldn't roll back down.

"It just needs some ice," I told Micah. Ice was a luxury in China, but we were lucky to have a few cubes left in our small freezer. And I wasn't going to the hospital until after I had a damn burger. The chill of the air against my knee as we drove back to the apartments brought some relief. By the time we got home, my entire knee was an angry hue of purple.

As I hobbled through the entryway of the apartments, my eyes locked onto the old broom that had been sitting outside a vacant apartment since I'd moved in with Micah.

"This!" I exclaimed. "It's perfect!"

I grabbed the broom and turned it upside down so the wooden handle planted firmly on the ground. I leaned my weight onto the broom.

"I can use it to walk," I said, proud of my makeshift cane.

"Just don't slip on the ice," Micah said, grabbing my elbow to help me balance.

Once inside, Micah put away the ground meat and helped me take off my shoes. The adrenaline had worn off by now, and bending my knee had become incredibly painful. We told each other "good night," laughing that it should really be "good morning," and retreated to our separate rooms. I slowly peeled my jeans off, then shuffled into bed naked, broom standing sentinel beside the bed. I slipped into sleep immediately.

When I woke up later than afternoon, Micah was already awake. "So, what are you going to do first, Anna, go to the hospital or make those burgers?" He laughed deeply.

I grinned back at him, "Hospital first, I think."

The following hours-long hospital ordeal left me with a

photo of broken cartilage from the x-ray machine, but the majority of the kneecap was still in place. I wouldn't need surgery, and I could expect swelling for a month. In the meantime, I'd need to stay off of the knee as much as possible. The hospital didn't have crutches, though. If I wanted those, I'd have to find a special shop and pay a surprisingly exorbitant amount. I decided to stick with my broom.

Later that evening, as our friends chattered on in the living room, I spooned pools of butter over inch-thick burger patties cooking in the frying pan. Micah stood beside me, slicing our finest cheeses to melt on top.

"These had better be some damn good burgers," he chuckled. And they were.

I Think I Need a Doctor

The sink was close enough to the toilet that I could rest my chin on its cold, white rim while still seated on my porcelain throne. What was happening to me was violent. Violent vomiting. Violent diarrhea. And it had been like this for the past three days. I didn't have a fever, though, and my body didn't hurt. I just couldn't keep any food down. And it was becoming increasingly difficult to keep water down, too.

Diarrhea was common in China. The water wasn't potable and food safety standards were practically non-existent. You couldn't trust that anyone handling your food had washed their hands, let alone kept the food at proper temperatures, and you didn't know if the lettuce you just bought was grown next to the gutter a few blocks away or if it came from the farmer in the next village over. And if it came from the farm, did they use human feces as fertilizer? There were plenty of reasons for foodborne illness.

I'd had consistent diarrhea for the past month. It wasn't bothering me too much, though, and I figured I just needed more probiotics in my diet. Or maybe I needed to cook at home more instead of eating out almost every night. Either way, many expats in Jinan experienced prolonged diarrhea, so I figured it was just my turn. But the vomiting was new, and I was puking so hard that I would pass out mid-regurgitation.

When I felt like I could safely exit the bathroom, I made my way to the spare bedroom and sprawled out on the bed. There were no windows in the living room, and my bedroom contained the sunroom, so the guest bedroom was the only place I could sit, or lay, in actual sunlight. The evening sun felt warm on my skin. My body felt… strange. I was clammy and sluggish. I didn't feel like I could think right. I decided to text my friend, Samm.

"*Samm, something isn't right,*" I wrote to her. "*Do you think I need to go to the hospital?*"

"*What's going on?*" she asked.

I told her about my recent troubles, and how for the past three days, things had gotten much worse.

"*Yeah, you should get that looked at sooner than later,*" she said. "*You should probably go now.*"

"*I'm so tired,*" I said, "*I'll take a nap then go when I wake up.*"

"*Okay, text me before you go,*" she said.

By the time I woke up, it was dark outside. I laid awake in bed for a couple of minutes before my body signaled it was time to expel liquid from both the front and back of me again. I ran to the bathroom. And then it happened, again and again. When I was done, I laid myself out on the bathroom floor, resting my cheek against the cold tile. I felt so weak, I didn't think I could move.

Then Alan came home. Alan was my Chinese ex-boyfriend. We were still living together even after breaking up due to the cost of living. It benefited us both to have the other around and paying half the bills. We were mostly amicable with each other, but Alan was just as happy to ignore me while he was home rather than pretend we were happy friends.

"What are you doing on the floor, Anna?" he asked, seemingly annoyed.

"I don't think I can get up. I keep puking everywhere. And I have diarrhea. I feel so weak," I told him.

"Then you need to go to the hospital," he said.

"I... I... want to go," I stammered, "but I really feel like I can't move." I felt like I wanted to cry, and my body shook, but there were no tears.

Alan sighed and said, "Fine, I'll take you. Let me help you up."

He slipped his arms under mine and pulled me up from the armpits until I was standing. I clung to him tight as he walked me towards the front door and down the apartment stairs, grabbing my purse as we exited the apartment.

"We'll take my motorbike," he said. "It'll be too hard to catch a taxi this time of night."

I didn't know how late it was, except that it must have been after 7:00 pm for it to be dark. Alan mounted his orange motorbike and held it steady as I climbed on behind him. He pulled his helmet over his head and started the engine. I didn't have a helmet, and I was too weak to sit straight up. I slumped over, resting my head on Alan's back between his shoulder blades, and we took off.

The drive to the hospital took twenty-minutes on a good day, and we had to stop twice so I could vomit. The second time, nothing actually came up, but the dry heaving was still painful. Alan had taken me to the second-largest hospital in Jinan since it was easier to navigate to. It practiced TCM, traditional Chinese medicine, alongside Western medicine. TCM relies on the five elements in the human body along with Yin and Yang, using herbal medicine, acupuncture, and other traditional, pre-laboratory tested practices. When we arrived I asked Alan to take charge of check-in and registration. I had to pay all visit fees upfront before I was allowed back into the hospital, and I paid extra to be expedited.

The waiting room for the night clinic was a narrow hallway lined with metal chairs. At the far end of the hallway was the nurses' station, and only a thin wall separated the waiting room from the large communal treatment room, which had patients in as many beds as possible with zero privacy. We sat in silence, but soon I had to rush to the bathroom. The nearest toilet was located in another section of the hospital, and getting to it meant walking – or in my case, running – down a dark corridor and through a set of double doors that would have been propped open during the day. The bathroom consisted of a single squatty-potty and a sink. I tried my best to aim accurately as the violence found me again.

To my surprise, I was only in the waiting room for approximately ten minutes. Getting expedited really paid off. The nurses called me into a small room and checked my vitals while I relayed my symptoms.

"We're going to need a stool sample. Do you think you can provide that?" the nurse asked.

I nodded, and the nurse handed me the necessary equipment. "Take it to the laboratory when you're done," she said.

It didn't take long before I needed to rush to the bathroom again, collecting the specimen with a tiny plastic scooper and open plastic cup. When I was finished, Alan helped me find the laboratory on the second floor before heading back to the nurses' station.

"Ah, good, you're finished," the nurse said. "The doctor just arrived."

As the doctor poked and prodded around my body, I felt myself turn cold and limp. Then I slumped over the chair to vomit, feeling as though I was choking despite nothing coming out. The doctor called for the nurse, and together they walked me from the room next to the nurses' station to the communal treatment room and ushered me onto a bed.

"You're extremely dehydrated," the doctor said. "We're going to need to give you an IV."

My vision faded to all white as I felt myself faint on the bed. At least I was laying down, but I wondered if I was in the process of dying.

I came to quickly as Alan shook me with both hands. The nurse and doctor were gone.

"The doctor is getting you an IV," Alan said, "and I'm going back home."

"What?" I asked weakly in surprise. "You're just going to leave me here?"

"You're not my girlfriend anymore, Anna, I don't have to stay with you," Alan told me coldly. "It's late and I have to work tomorrow."

"I don't want to be here alone," I whimpered. Chinese hospitals were not very patient-focused, and you were expected to do basically everything by yourself or have your family help you. If you're cold, your family brings blankets. If you're hungry, your family brings food. The hospital just provides the bed and the medicine.

"Can you call Samm for me?" I asked. Samm was my best friend from university, and her dorms were only ten minutes away from the hospital.

Alan sighed, "Fine, give me your phone."

With great effort, I dug my phone out of my purse and handed it to Alan. I didn't have the wherewithal to dial on my own – it was a struggle just trying to talk. All I wanted to do was close my eyes again. The organs in my body felt heavy, but my limbs felt like they were floating.

"She's coming," Alan told me as he slid the phone next to me on the bed, "and I'm leaving. See you at home." And with that, Alan left.

I could speak the language better than Samm, but she was quickly catching up. Usually, I was the one taking other foreigners to the hospital – nobody liked navigating the Chinese medical system alone – but now it was me that needed help. I knew Samm would come, and I knew she would stay with me for as long as was needed. I told myself that all I needed to do was wait for Samm. She could talk to the doctors. She could translate. She could let my parents know if I died.

Then the doctor and two nurses appeared with two large IV bags that looked like they were about to burst from their seams.

"Okay, are you ready?" asked the doctor as he held the IV needle up for me to see.

"Blood makes me faint," I blurted out, "and so does getting an IV in." I was feeling a bit frantic. "Please don't put it in my elbow pit! Please put it up top instead!" I had great, accessible veins on the outside of my arms, and I'd learned back home that if you asked the nurses to stick the needles there, they usually would. At least I was already laying down, but I didn't want to pass out again.

The doctor grabbed one of my arms while the nurse grabbed the other. They wrapped a rubber strip around each arm to make the veins pop. They slapped my skin. They repositioned the rubber strips. They murmured to each other, but I couldn't understand what they were saying. Then the doctor moved to my cubital fossa and began pressing his thumb into my veins. I squeezed my eyes shut, anticipating the needle. My elbow pits were highly sensitive areas for me when it came to needles. In fact, just thinking about drawing blood from there, or needles under the skin at all, makes me lightheaded. Then the doctor said something to the nurse, and they both stopped prodding me.

"What's your name?" asked the doctor.

"Anna," I told him.

"Anna, I'm very sorry," the doctor said, "but you're so dehydrated that your veins have all sunken. They're too deep to get a needle into. We're going to have to put the IV into your wrists." He turned my hand over so my palms faced up and rubbed the veins on my exposed wrist. I began to cry.

"Please, no," I begged, "anywhere but there, please!"

"We really have no other option. You'll be okay, don't worry. We'll be quick," the nurse at my other arm told me.

I let out a moan and felt a single hot tear stream down my face. It was then that I realized that despite my crying, that was the first tear to actually leave my eyes. The nurse and the doctor each grabbed a wrist at the same time, and they began working to get the needles in. I clenched my teeth as hard as I clenched my eyes and tried to sing myself a song in my head as a distraction. Finally, it was over, but the room began to spin as I looked down to examine my wrists.

I took a deep breath and moved my vision from my wrists to the IV tubing. One line dangling from each arm, the tubing snaked up and around two metal IV bag holders.

"You can go home when these bags are done," the doctor said, and then the team left.

As I looked around the communal treatment room, I saw that most people were staring at me. The only ones who weren't were those in active pain, lying in their beds moaning or surrounded by their families as they labored in their agony. I tried to lay as still as possible in the bed. Any movement of the hands sent an unpleasant sensation through my wrists that made me want to faint all over again. I don't know how long it was before Samm showed up, but it wasn't too long after inserting the IV.

"Oh my God, Anna, you look awful," Samm said as she found a chair to pull next to my bed. "What on Earth happened? And where's Alan?"

I told her about my symptoms and the diagnosis of dehydration, but as I was explaining Alan's departure, I felt an emergency brewing in my bowels.

"Samm," I said frantically, "I'm about to have diarrhea, but I can't make it to the bathroom by myself with these two IVs hooked up to me."

Samm's eyes grew wide when she realized what I was asking her to do. "I'll take you to the bathroom, Anna. Come on, we'll take it slow."

"We can't be too slow," I said. "I'm going to mess myself."

A nurse passed by as Samm was helping me off the bed.

"Excuse me, nurse, is there a closer bathroom? The one down the hall is too far away, she can't make it, she has diarrhea," Samm said.

"There's another one next to the doctor's room. You can use that one," the nurse said, and pointed towards a closed door with her chin.

We made it to the restroom just in time, but Samm had to help me pull down my pants and underwear. I couldn't bend my wrists with IVs in them. Luckily, this toilet was a western toilet, and I was able to sit comfortably. I felt so embarrassed as I released my bowels in front of Samm, but she had to stay to hold the IVs. Nothing came out, though. I felt the sensation of having diarrhea without actually having diarrhea.

"Nothings coming out, Samm," I groaned.

"I noticed," Samm said with a chuckle.

I had one more thing to ask, though. "Samm… I can't… with this needle in my wrist… I can't wipe. I just can't. The IV is in the way and it hurts." I really had tried to wipe on my own, but I just couldn't do it.

"Oh, you are SO lucky I am such a good friend," Samm said, and reached for my toilet paper. As she wiped my ass, I believe that both of us were thankful nothing had actually come out.

She helped me get my clothes back on and walked me back to the bed. But as soon as I managed to climb back up, the urge to go hit again. "Samm," I cried, "it's happening again!"

In total, Samm took me back to the bathroom six times that night, wiping my ass for me each time. Nothing ever came out. Eventually, my stomach settled, and my eyelids grew heavy.

"You can sleep if you want," Samm told me. I was relieved to hear her say so, and let myself drift off.

Suddenly, Samm was shaking me awake. "Anna, the doctor is here."

A new shift had started at the hospital, and a new doctor was here to examine me.

"How are you feeling?" the doctor asked.

"Still awful," I told her. "I feel so weak. There's no diarrhea coming out, but I keep having to go. I feel like I'm sinking into sand."

The doctor pushed on my skin in a few places, then examined my IVs.

"*Aiya*, the flow on these is way too low!" she exclaimed. "These should have run dry hours ago, no wonder you still feel bad."

She fiddled with the IVs, and I felt a coldness flow into my veins. As the doctor walked away, I let myself drift back off to sleep. When I woke back up, an hour had passed, and the IV bags were empty. Samm sat beside me browsing on her phone.

"Thank you for coming here, Samm," I told her.

She looked up and smiled at me. "You're my friend, it's what I'm here for," she said.

Eventually, the doctor came back. She pushed down on my arm and watched the skin rise. I closed my eyes as she removed the IVs from my wrists, and kept looking away as she wrapped a gauze bandage around them to keep the needle holes from bleeding.

"You're still a little dehydrated," the doctor said, "but I'm discharging you anyway. Here, take this home and make sure you drink it before you go to bed. This will get you back to normal."

Then she handed me a small white packet filled with some form of granular medicine. I could read the word for "salt" on the packet's label. These were oral rehydration salts.

"I have the results from your stool sample, too," she continued. "You have gastroenteritis. Basically, all of the good bacteria in your gut has died. You only have bad bacteria left, and your body can't handle it. You need to eat some yogurt to get your good bacteria back."

"Thank you, doctor," I told her. "I'll take the medicine and get some yogurt."

"Make sure you mix the salts with hot water, not cold water. That's bad for your stomach. You should feel better in a few days," she said. "You're free to go home now." And with that, she left my bedside and made her way to the next patient.

I was feeling so much better now after the IVs. I could walk normally, and I felt neither like I was floating nor like I was too heavy. Before leaving, I translated the characters on the IV bags.

"Glucose," they read. Samm and I left the hospital, hoping a taxi wouldn't be too hard to find. Taxis tended to loiter around the hospitals, so it didn't take us too long to hail one down.

"You take this one, I'll catch the next one," Samm told me.

I hugged her tight, "Thank you, Samm. Thank you so much for staying with me. It just sucks being in the hospital alone."

"I'm just repaying the kindness, really," she said. "And next time, you'll be the one helping *me*."

I climbed into the taxi and gave directions to my apartment. Alan was asleep by the time I got home, so I quietly put the tea kettle on to warm up the water for my salts. The instructions on the oral rehydration salts package said to mix with 800 ml of water, and drink the whole thing. I let the water come to a full boil and dissolved the salts, but waited thirty minutes before trying to drink it. I had a sensitive mouth and still wasn't accustomed to drinking hot things, even tea. It seemed like the Chinese had the superpower of being able to drink boiling hot things without being scalded. A superpower that I completely lacked. When the oral solution was gone, I toddled off to the bathroom to pee for what I realized was the first time in the entire day. Then I climbed into bed, exhausted, and fell asleep while reading up on gastroenteritis on my phone.

I never could suss out exactly what food wrecked me so thoroughly, and there was no point in being cautious about what I put in my mouth. Food safety was practically nonexistent in China. Just because a restaurant was clean didn't mean the food was sanitary, and my Chinese coworkers chalked my experience up to "something that just happens".

* * *

I was far from the only foreigner with medical issues, though. Poor Micah had a full-blown surgery. Micah and I were roommates for a time, and while we were living together, he had taken up practicing Tai Kwan Do with a few other foreigners at a local studio. Being dropped repeatedly on the floor made his back hurt, though, and he routinely came home slumped. Still, he enjoyed the martial art, and kept at it despite the pain.

Except the pain never went away. In fact, it grew worse and worse as the weeks went by. Soon, Micah wasn't able to walk without pain. Then he wasn't able to walk with his back straight at all. Still, he persisted through the pain thanks to some strong over-the-counter painkillers from the local pharmacy. A few weeks later, Micah's back hurt when sitting, too. And the pain only worsened. He was teaching English at one of the local universities in the city, which required a fair amount of sitting, only exacerbating his problem. Soon, he was popping pain pills every hour on the hour. They weren't strong enough to be considered a narcotic, but they were much stronger than anything we could find back home. Still, the pain bled through every pill.

Eventually, Micah had had enough. It had been months since his back had first started hurting, but now all he could manage to do was lie down to find relief. He was walking stooped over like a little old man, and required the use of a cane for support. When he finally took himself to the doctor for an x-ray, he was told that he had broken three vertebrae in his back, from L1 to L3. He had literally been walking around with a broken back. The doctor he saw told him he usually saw this injury in sixty-year-old men, not strapping young lads, and that he needed an immediate surgery.

Micah didn't have time for surgery, though. He needed to make it through the semester first. His boss was hesitant to wait, telling Micah he would put up the funds for the surgery if he got it sooner rather than later, but Micah refused stating that the students were relying on him to finish out the class. He could make it the last two weeks, he insisted.

When the school semester finished at the start of the Spring Festival holiday, Micah agreed to the surgery, although he was determined to go alone. His Chinese was good enough, and he could translate what he didn't understand with his phone. Besides, everyone else was either traveling or enjoying the start of the holiday. He arrived at the hospital early in the morning on a weekday, and was taken to meet the doctor in his office.

"You're the only one I'm treating today," the doctor told him, "and this is a relatively uncommon technique. I'm the only surgeon in the city who can do this."

"Is there anything I need to be worried about?" Micah asked. He felt worried about everything.

"Well, we need to keep you awake during the procedure. Don't worry, you won't be able to feel your back, but we need to be able to tell if we've hit a wrong nerve or done any other damage."

Micah swallowed hard. Awake? That sounded terrifying, but he didn't really have any other options, not if he wanted his back fixed. "Fine," Micah said, "I can do that."

They led Micah to a communal treatment room and showed him his bed. The four other people in the room all stared at him. Micah was Black, and Black people were gawked at relentlessly in Jinan. He was instructed to take off his shoes and shirt before sitting on the bed.

"We need you to sit up as straight as possible," said the anesthesiologist as he walked towards Micah, needle in hand.

Micah straightened, though not without pain, and held his breath as the anesthesiologist pushed the small needle into his back, delivering a spinal block. Then the anesthesiologist helped him lay on the bed face down before the spinal block took effect. Then the doctor came over, his assistant wheeling a tray of long, intimidating looking pins beside him.

"I'm going to put these in now," the doctor said. "You need to hold as still as possible. Don't move, or else you could get hurt, okay?"

"Okay," Micah said nervously, and held his breath.

He didn't feel any pain as the doctor pushed the fore-arm-length needles into his back, tucking against his three broken vertebrae, but he could feel the pressure. The needles pinched and squeezed as they entered his flesh, though not in a torturous way.

"Now we take you to surgery," the doctor said, and beckoned for the nurses to help him wheel Micah's bed down the hallway and into the operating room.

Inside the operating room were more pins and a small hammer lying on a table in the middle of the room, underneath a series of floodlights. A TV had been placed on the table, as well.

"We're going to use a little microscopic camera to see your vertebrae on the TV," the doctor said excitedly. "You'll be able to watch the whole procedure." Micah wasn't sure how he felt about that. Should he be terrified or invigorated by watching his own operation?

The nurses parked the bed under the floodlights, and Micah gingerly turned his head towards the TV.

"Make sure you hold still now, okay? We're going to start. It should take about three hours," the doctor said, and moved out of Micah's line of sight.

Micah felt hands on his body, then more pressure and the sensation of a squeeze. The doctor's assistant turned on the TV, and there was the live footage of one of his vertebrae. He wasn't even sure how the camera got in there. Then he heard a soft "tink tink tink" sound as the doctor began gently hammering on one of the pins in his back. He saw the pin on the TV sink deeper and deeper into his body, disappearing below the bone. He felt a cough well up in his throat, and had to swallow hard to keep it at bay, not wanting to move his body more than what it took to breathe.

Micah put all of his focus into laying still. The tinking was constant, and almost soothing, and if he weren't terrified for his life, he almost could have slept. When he needed a break, he would allow his eyes to stare at the TV, watching as the pins slowly repositioned his bones back into their proper place. His arms fell asleep, and his neck hurt, but he wouldn't allow himself to move even the slightest centimeter. He just needed to focus and breathe.

The operation took all of three hours, and Micah let out a huge sigh of relief as he watched the doctor remove the long pins from his back on the TV. He still had no feeling, but he could no longer sense pressure, either. The procedure was over, and he'd survived. The nurses wheeled his bed back to the communal treatment room, and Micah allowed himself to fall asleep.

He woke up to a dozen missed calls and twice as many text messages, all from friends concerned that they hadn't heard from him since he'd gone into the hospital. He responded to the texts one by one, still lying on his stomach. He would need to lay like that for three days while the wound was still fresh. But now, he was hungry. He really didn't want to bother anyone, but he knew that the only way he could get food was if someone else brought it to him. So, before the surgery, he'd gathered a small group of people to help him. Those that came were not necessarily his closest and dearest friends in Jinan, but rather the people who he knew had the time and financial stability to go out of their way on his behalf. With his stomach growling, he messaged a fellow university teacher about getting a meal, though he really hated to trouble his friend.

Micah was flipped from his stomach to his back on the fourth day of recovery. He would still need another week's stay in the hospital, but at least he had a bit more mobility, and he could sit up on his own now. He was happy to discover that the pain was gone. He was still in pain from the procedure, sure, but it wasn't the same type of deep pain that resulted from his broken back.

He decided to allow visitors now, sending out texts with his address and a small list of items he was allowed to eat and drink, knowing his friends wouldn't come empty handed. Luckily, some-one had brought him a bag of clothes the day prior, although he still wasn't strong enough to put them on. A Chinese friend had brought a blanket, too, worried that Micah would get cold at nights. He was very grateful for that.

A steady stream of visitors appeared over the next week. Most people only visited once, but he had enough friends in the city that there was always somebody in the room. At nights, the other men in the other beds would talk with him, asking him questions about his life back home and his time in Jinan. He formed a friendship with one old man in particular who had been in the hospital before Micah arrived and didn't look like he would be leaving any time soon.

Priscilla and I had a bottle of wine ready for Micah when he got home. Seeing him walk upright through the door was like watching the transformation from a caterpillar into a butterfly. His smile was huge, and his back was straight. The surgery was a success. He immediately loaded a DVD into the disc player next to the TV. The doctor had given him a copy of the procedure recording, and Priscilla and I watched in fascination as Micah narrated the surgery to us.

"You know, I never would have been able to afford this surgery in the United States," Micah reflected once the video was over, "I guess it's a good thing this happened in Jinan." Curious, we looked up the cost of Micah's surgery. What would have cost over $300,000 USD, Micah received for the equivalent of $5,600 USD. What a steal!

* * *

As scary as surgery is, at least Micah's issues and procedures were easy to diagnose and (relatively) easy to treat. I can't say we all had the same experience, however, as Kelley found out after a night on the town. Kelley was Samm's roommate. They both came to China as foreign exchange students from the same university in New York, and while they were just acquaintances upon their arrival, they found they had a lot in common and became fast friends. At the start of their second semester, they asked to be placed in the same dorm room, which made their space a prime hang-out spot for the rest of the friend's group after classes were over.

It was a Friday night, and Kelley and Samm had gone out drinking with a few Korean friends. They had a nice meal before starting their night, but not even a full stomach could protect you from the potency of baijiu, China's liquor of choice. Most foreigners found baijiu hard to stomach. It was certainly an acquired taste, but you had to get used to it quickly if you had local friends, business affairs, or were considered an honored guest somewhere.

The Koreans were seasoned drinkers, and often told stories of their grandmothers drinking them under the table at dinner. Kelley was trying to keep up, while Samm was trying to slow down. By midnight, they had killed the bottle of baijiu and were ready to make their way back to the dorms. But Kelley was parched, and she knew she needed water if she wanted to soften the next day's hangover. The street food vendors were still out in full force, serving the late-night weekend crowds that constantly streamed in and out of the bars and barbeque halls. Kelley found a vendor selling water, bought a bottle, and downed half of it on the walk home.

But when Kelley woke up late the next morning, she couldn't see! Her world was completely black. Something was terribly wrong.

"Samm!" she cried out. "Samm, I can't see anything!"

"What do you mean you can't see anything," Samm asked as she stirred from her bed. "Like your vision is blurry?"

"No, like I can't see anything!" Kelley exclaimed. "I'm blind!"

"How the hell can you be blind?!" Samm questioned, trying not to panic.

"I don't know," Kelley answered. "I could see when we got home last night. All I had was baijiu and water."

Samm got out of bed and found Kelley's half-empty bottle of water. She untwisted the cap and gave it a sniff.

"Kelley, this water smells funny," she said. "Actually, it smells like the tap water!"

Tap water in China had a distinguishable smell to it, and was full of bacteria and heavy metals. You could boil the bacteria out, sure, but there was nothing that could be done about the metals, and the smell lingered even after being boiled.

"You don't think that guy gave me tap water, do you?" Kelley questioned, "Could that make me go blind like this?"

"I don't know," Samm said. "I mean, we've all heard that baijiu can make you go blind, but that's just a myth, right? That doesn't actually happen, or people would be blind all the time. Right? Right?"

They weren't going to get any answers just by staying in their dorm, however. They needed to get Kelley to the hospital. University students didn't have much money, though, and all the hospitals required payment upfront to be seen or treated. Luckily, the university issued insurance to all its foreign students. If only Samm could find the paperwork...

She did find it, eventually, although the details were sparse. She found the information about the policy number, but discovered that university students were only covered at one particular hospital, and it only practiced TCM. They didn't have time to worry about that, though, they just needed to get Kelley there. Samm helped Kelley dress and guided her out of the dorms. The hospital was within walking distance, but neither of them wanted to attempt the busy sidewalks that were crammed full of people on a weekend. Samm hailed a taxi instead, and slowly guided Kelley inside.

They arrived at the hospital in a few short minutes, and Samm helped Kelley up the steps, into the building, and onto a chair near the registration desk. She registered Kelley, handing over the insurance information and paying the registration fee. Treatment was covered by insurance, but you still had to pay to see the doctor.

"The ophthalmology department is on the fourth floor," the lady behind the desk told Samm, "But the elevator is broken, so you'll have to take the stairs."

Samm returned to Kelley. "You're going to have to walk up some stairs now," she said.

"How many?" Kelley asked hesitantly.

"Four flights," said Samm, and Kelley let out an exasperated moan.

Samm wrapped her arm around Kelley's back and guided her to the stairs. She placed Kelley's hand on the rail, and Kelley took a step up. As she began to make her way up the stairs, Kelley began to feel just how bad her hangover was. Her head was pounding. Her body was shaky. She wasn't well, and it was hitting her hard.

"Samm, I don't think I can make it up there," she said in a low voice, unsure of what to do.

"Oh yes you will," Samm said. "You're not just going to be blind in the lobby. Here, hang onto me."

Kelley leaned hard on Samm as Samm wrapped both arms around her. Kelley let her weight fall on Samm, and Samm dug deep within herself to carry her up the stairs. They stopped to rest at every landing so Samm could catch her breath and Kelley could regain her bearings. Eventually, they reached the fourth floor. Samm sat Kelley in a chair, then walked the registration paperwork over to the nurses' station.

The hospital was quiet for a Saturday, and they were called into the doctor's office rather quickly. Samm walked Kelley into the room and sat her in a wooden chair next to a hospital bed. Neither had been in China for very long, and they struggled trying to understand the questions the doctor was asking. Both parties practiced a bit of patience as Samm and Kelley tried to explain their prior night's activities and what Kelley was currently experiencing. Samm watched the doctor shine a light in Kelley's eyes over and over again. Kelley couldn't see the light at all.

"We're going to have to admit you," said the doctor. "We'll start treatment right away. You've been eating too many cold things, and your blood has gone bad, that's why you're blind. We have to stimulate the blood flow again."

Neither Samm nor Kelley really knew what that meant, and the explanation certainly didn't come from western medicine. Still, this was the only help they were going to get, so Samm led Kelley behind the doctor and into a communal treatment room. They positioned Kelley on a bed, and then the doctor left.

A group of nurses arrived a few minutes later carrying a tray of tiny needles.

"This is acupuncture," one of the nurses explained. "We need you to take off your shoes and socks. This will help cleanse your blood."

Samm removed Kelley's shoes and socks, and the nurses got to work. While one nurse pushed the tiny needles into Kelley's feet, another went to work around her eyes. A needle in her forehead, two more on the sides of her eyes. There were needles in her arm, too, and scattered around her body, although there were a dozen needles in her feet. She wiggled her toes in curiosity, but couldn't feel the needles. At least they didn't hurt.

"We'll come back in an hour, you rest now," said one of the nurses.

Kelley's stomach was starting to hurt. She was hungry and feeling dehydrated from her hangover. Samm volunteered to fetch her a meal and some water, and Kelley tried to nap while Samm was away. She was feeling better by the time the nurses returned, belly full of egg and green onion dumplings, washed down with bottled water from a trusted source.

"Any better?" a nurse asked.

"No," said Kelley, "I still can't see anything."

"*Ai*," the nurse sighed, "we'll have to try again later. In a few hours. Here, drink this now." She handed Samm a hot cup of what looked like tea and smelled like medicine.

"What's in it?" Samm asked, but couldn't understand a word

of what the nurse rattled off.

Samm guided Kelley's hands around the cup, and Kelley took a sip.

"How does it taste?" Samm asked Kelley, wrinkling her nose.

"It tastes… like herbs and licorice. And bitter. It's definitely traditional medicine," Kelley said, trying her best to get the drink down her throat as fast as possible without burning her mouth.

Kelley spent the rest of the day and through the evening undergoing round after round of acupuncture and medicinal tea. Samm stayed with her the entire time, leaving only to fetch food. Helping Kelley navigate the squatty-potty bathrooms while blind proved a challenge. One wrong move, and your foot was in the toilet. A few inches off center, and you're peeing on the floor.

By the time night fell, Kelley was still blind, but her hangover was gone, and she was feeling physically better. Samm couldn't stay overnight, though, and left for the dorms around 10:00 pm. Kelley struggled to find sleep that night, listening to the breathing and moaning of the other patients in the room with her. Eventually, she fell into a dreamless sleep that lasted until morning.

As the morning sun filtered into the hospital room, Kelley opened her eyes and looked around the facility. The families of some of the other patients had already gathered by their bedsides, despite the early morning hour. It was then that Kelley realized she was seeing again! She was looking at those people, and she *saw* them. Her vision had returned! The nurses were delighted at her improvement when they came to check on her, stating the importance of clean blood. The acupuncture had worked, they declared, and Kelley was cleared to be discharged.

Samm returned to Kelley shortly afterwards, relieved to see her friend was better.

"I did some research last night," Samm said. "Both heavy metals and dehydration from drinking can cause temporary blindness. I think that's what happened to you, between the baijiu and the tap water…"

"That makes a lot more sense than having bad blood from eating too many cold things," Kelley mused.

Was it the acupuncture that cured Kelley of her blindness? Did the medicinal tea help? Or was it the rest and rehydration that led to the recovery of her eyesight? Perhaps a little of everything helped make her better, but the next time Kelley needed the hospital, she opted for one that practiced Western medicine.

* * *

Medical treatment in China was cheap, at least, but it didn't always come easy. Priscilla discovered this one time during an asthma attack. Deep in the heart of winter, the coal-burning steam power plants used to heat the city were running at full force, pumping out endless plumes of smoke. The city of Jinan was surrounded by mountains on three sides, creating a bowl that the dust and pollution swirled around perpetually. The smog choked the city during winter, and on this day the pollution index was well over 500 ppm. For reference, an air quality value of 300 ppm is considered hazardous to human health.

Priscilla wasn't surprised that the asthma attack happened, considering the state of the air and the fact she'd been running around all day, but she wasn't expecting her inhaler to not work. She called me late in the afternoon, her voice tinged with panic.

"Anna, I can't breathe," she said, "my inhaler isn't working. I need to get a nebulizer from the hospital. Can you go with me to translate?"

"Absolutely," I said, and asked which hospital she would prefer.

This wasn't Priscilla's first rodeo with a Chinese hospital — she'd been sick enough before to need intervention, and while she was there, she'd made friends with a doctor who spoke English. We'd been sending all our friends to request that doctor if they couldn't speak Chinese, much to the doctor's enjoyment. Priscilla texted her, wondering if she was working a shift that evening, but received no response. No matter, we would head to the same hospital, and maybe we would get lucky. If not, at least I spoke the language.

We registered without trouble and took our spots in the waiting room. When the nurse called her back to be examined, I explained about Priscilla's asthma, that her inhaler wasn't working, and that she needed a nebulizer.

"She doesn't need a nebulizer," the nurse said. "It's not that serious."

"But her inhaler isn't helping her," I protested. "She can't breathe."

"It's just allergies," the nurse insisted. "She just needs to stay inside today."

I relayed what the nurse said to Priscilla. "No," she said, "this is NOT allergies! I can hardly breathe!" She pulled out her inhaler to show the nurse.

"Look, she really does have asthma," I said, pointing to the inhaler, "and she's in pain."

"Tell her I know my body and I know what I need," Priscilla insisted.

I did so, emphasizing the point that she's had this issue before and knows how to treat it.

"You're not a doctor," the nurse said. "I know what allergies look like. If it's not allergies, then it's the smog. Go home and stay inside."

I translated for Priscilla. "No!" she cried, "I need help! I NEED a nebulizer."

"Are you okay with taking a stand?" I asked Priscilla, turning her way.

"I'll do anything necessary to breathe," she said.

I turned to the nurse. "We aren't leaving this room until the doctor looks at her," I said, furrowing my brow and widening my stance.

The nurse glared at me, but said nothing before exiting the room. She returned a few minutes later, trailing behind the doctor. I was expecting her to put up more of a fight about the situation.

"My nurse says you refuse to leave," the doctor said. "What's going on?"

I told the doctor about the asthma, the inhaler, the difficulty breathing, and the request for a nebulizer. I insisted it wasn't allergies. Maybe the smog had caused the asthma attack, but she couldn't just go home and sit it out. The doctor pulled out his stethoscope and listened to Priscilla's chest. Then he listened to her back. Then he listened to her chest again.

"Well, it's definitely an asthma attack," the doctor said. "You said her inhaler didn't help right? In that case, she'll need a nebulizer."

I glanced at the nurse, who was glaring at Priscilla while the doctor retrieved the breathing treatment. The doctor set Priscilla up in a chair in the waiting room, nebulizer flowing, and told Priscilla to breathe through the mask for twenty minutes. I sat with her, playing on my phone while she focused on getting back to normal. The nurse never stopped glaring at us. I don't think she was used to patients advocating for themselves. But the next time Priscilla needed a nebulizer, she received treatment right away.

If You Can't Stand the Heat

Tacos. All we wanted were tacos. Do you know how hard it is to get tacos in Jinan? The closest Mexican restaurant was all the way in Beijing, and even then, the food was a crapshoot. Sure, that picture of a burrito with guacamole and sour cream looks great, but when it comes out you discover that your guacamole is wasabi and your sour cream is mayonnaise. We were going to have to make our own tacos, which meant a trip to the downtown mall for the foreign goods store.

We found the last package of flour tortillas and grabbed it up greedily. Then we made for the sour cream. You could make your own sour cream at home out of plain yogurt and a lemon, but it paled in comparison to the store-bought brands. This one came from Australia. Then we picked out a small block of sharp yellow cheese. It came from Australia, too. Did the store have black olives? It did? Hallelujah! The tomatoes, lettuce, and onion we could pick up at the wet market, and the ground beef we would get from Da Run Fa (a superstore chain similar to Wal-Mart).

Micah and I invited Priscilla over for dinner. It was the middle of the Spring Festival, and she had just gotten back from a trip to the Philippines. She'd fallen ill, though, catching a nasty cold halfway through the trip, and was now curled up on our couch, tucked under her heavy winter coat. Micah sat next to her as she regaled us with stories from her overseas excursion, and I busied myself in the kitchen with the ground beef.

Our kitchen was far from clean. We weren't filthy animals—we cleaned our dishes and we wiped down the counters—but we neglected everything else. In China, you *really* needed to clean your kitchen well, especially if you were cooking local dishes. Chinese food uses a lot of oil. A LOT of oil. And despite each kitchen coming equipped with an oil guard behind the stovetop, oil would crack and pop and splatter everywhere around the room. If you weren't on top of it, it would coat everything, and it would stay on the counters even when wiping away spilled food. We never cleaned the oil.

I was chopping a tomato when I smelled the ground beef start to burn. *Not today*, I thought to myself, and hurried to turn down the stove and stir around the beef. I stirred a bit too aggressively, a bit too carelessly, enough that a chunk of beef and a small puddle of grease spilled out of the pan and rolled into the fire of the gas stove. Before I knew what was happening, the grease caught fire. I jerked the pan back, but it was too late, and the grease in the pan caught fire, too!

"MICAH!" I shouted as I dropped the pan back on the stove. "Micah, there's fire!!!"

I wasn't sure if he could hear me through the closed sliding glass door that separated the kitchen and sunroom from the rest of the apartment.

"Micah!" I yelled again as I tried not to panic, looking around the kitchen for something to smother the flames with. Finding nothing, I thought if I could get the flaming pan to the sink, I could contain the fire long enough to extinguish it. Maybe I could drown the grease in the water, I thought.

Micah burst through the kitchen door as I grabbed for the pan. I wasn't expecting the handle to be so hot, but the fire had heated that, too. I cried out, gripping the pan as best as I could while I took the three steps over to the sink, but the heat was too much to bear, and I dropped the pan. The pan clanged against the metal of the sink, and meat and grease went everywhere.

Micah and I stared in horror as the grease fire escalated up the kitchen wall. The building was made entirely out of concrete, which had been painted a pale shade of yellow, and now somehow it was on fire. All that grease we'd neglected to clean had gathered on the walls, and caught ablaze as I dropped the pan, sending the fire flying up the painted concrete, eagerly consuming the grease.

"IS THAT A FIRE?!" I heard Priscilla scream from the living room.

I realized in horror that there were exactly zero fire extinguishers in the apartment building, and that if we didn't get this fire out quick, the whole place could burn. It didn't quite register at the time that a concrete building wouldn't actually burn down. I abandoned Micah, running to the living room to find a blanket or towel or anything we could use to try and smother the fire. Micah was quicker than I was, though, and reached for a tea towel hidden under our empty coffee cups on the kitchen table.

"I got this! I got this!" he hollered from the kitchen as Priscilla and I waited anxiously in the living room.

I wasn't sure if I should go back in and help, or if I should be prepared to run for the fire department a block away. I stood frozen, muscles tightening yet refusing to move, watching the reflection from the fire shine through the kitchen door. Micah took the tea towel and began to whip the flames. THWAP! THWAP! THWAP! We heard Micah slam the towel against the kitchen walls and counters. THWAP! THWAP! Then we heard him let out a feral cry.

"I got it!" he shouted after a few moments. "It's out! It's out!"

Priscilla and I rushed back into the kitchen. Micah was leaning over the sink, sweat on his brow, breathing heavily with a scorched towel in his hand. Dark black marks ran up the wall, and for the first time, we noticed the thick cloud of smoke that hung in the air.

"Are you okay? Jesus, Micah, you really saved us!" I said.

"I'm fine. It's good, we're all good," Micah panted.

Priscilla began opening all the doors and windows in the apartment. We were on the bottom floor, and the smoke had already begun filtering out of the apartment and up the stairwell.

"I don't think we're gonna have tacos tonight, guys," I said, and we all laughed.

It took hours for the smoke to fully dissipate, and as the other foreign teachers came home, they wandered into our apartment inquiring about the smoke and smell.

"Don't worry," Priscilla told them, "we just almost burned the place down is all."

We scrubbed the kitchen clean after that, and made a point to keep up with the grease. We were never able to find a fire extinguisher for purchase, however, and we often wondered just how bad the fire would have been if it weren't for Micah's quick thinking. All we wanted were tacos.

Love in the Time of WiFi: The True Love Network

When I converted to Islam, I cut off my dreadlocks. It wasn't that dreadlocks were forbidden, but I felt that my ten-year journey with them had come to an end, and a new beginning meant new hair. I cried when I cut them off, my roommate, Micah, holding my hand the entire time. Micah had once had dreadlocks, too, and vividly recalled to me the day his brothers helped him cut his off years prior. My dreadlocks had been a part of my identity in China, and they were always a great conversation piece, especially since I was a white girl.

I now had a mere two inches of hair left on my head, a stark contrast to my former waist-long locks. I kept banging my head on the wall as I leaned against it, still not used to being without my previous home-grown padding. But it was easier to wear my headscarves now, and much easier to perform the daily washing rituals since I didn't have to worry about my hair not drying properly between washes.

I had more headscarves than any of my Chinese Muslim friends. Once I discovered how cheap I could find them on TaoBao (the Chinese version of E-Bay), I went crazy purchasing as many different patterns, styles, and colors as possible to match my everyday outfits and bring out a little bit of flare and fashion. I had everything from the standard black lace pullover hijab to long, elegant rainbow leopard print patterned scarves. My Hui friends had also introduced me to the jeweled clips one could pin on the hijab and flower puffs one could fasten to the back of one's head to give the illusion of more volume in the headscarf. I was there for all of it.

Looking back now, I can see that I converted to Islam as a way to deal with a major traumatic event. I thought it was the only chance at redemption I'd have after a tumultuous relationship with a Hui yak herder who turned out to be a narcissist and psychopath. But after the trauma, I was subconsciously trying to recreate the relationship, or rather, the perfect version of that relationship that I so badly wanted. I couldn't see that at the time, though. At the time, all I knew was that I was lonely in my heart and wanted to be with someone.

I didn't necessarily want to date someone in Jinan, though. I'd fallen in love with western China, and the Qinghai-Tibetan Plateau was calling to me. I wanted to move to Qinghai, truly, and was only planning on staying in Jinan for another year to save up my finances before relocating across the country. So, it wouldn't do much good to get into a relationship with a local, and I knew better than to date another foreigner. It always made the group dynamics awkward when an expat couple split. But a couple of my friends were having success with the new online dating scene that was emerging. I knew that all the mobile apps were mainly just for hookups, but surely there had to be a website for actual dating.

I opened my laptop, navigating to Baidu, China's main search engine. I typed "online dating" in Chinese and hit the search button. The first result to pop up was called "*Zhen Ai Wang*", the True Love Network. I clicked on the link and scrolled through the website. It boasted over 120 million registered users and was free to join, so I thought I'd give it a try.

Unedited Author's Proof

I needed an official ID to sign up, specifically a personal ID number. Every person in China had a number, similar to a social security number, and everyone had their number memorized. You needed it for most online stores, purchasing plane and train tickets, opening a bank account, and so on. Luckily, there was usually an option for foreigners to use their passport number, and Zhen Ai Wang followed suit. I filled out the profile information as best as I could, selecting "foreign" under the "ethnicity" option. Age: 24. Hometown: United States. Current Location: Jinan. Occupation: Teacher. I added mountain climbing, singing, playing the guitar, and reading as my hobbies. Mountain climbing in China meant more-so walking up giant hills and cliffs rather than scaling actual mountains, and is considered a common pastime equivalent to hiking. Then I uploaded three photos, two of me in a hijab, one a deep purple and the other a silky red, and one showing my ultra short hair with a blue and pink scarf around my neck. In Chinese Islam, I didn't need to wear a headscarf until I was married, so I could show my hair without issue.

Next it was time for me to choose my own preferences. I selected an age range of anyone twenty to thirty-five years old. For the location preferences, I selected both Qinghai and Tibet, but decided to leave out Xinjiang as I didn't think the location as beautiful. The website then asked me to select the preferred ethnicities of people I wanted to date. I selected Hui, Manchurian, Tibetan, Salar, Tu… all except for Han. I knew I was going to be objectified on this website, with people reaching out to date me just because I was exotic and white. So, I was going to treat my potential matches the same way. Plus, I figured someone who was Han would be much less likely to accept my new religious practices. I didn't set specific preferences for height, weight, religion, or level of education. And I noted that the website didn't ask for information like hair and eye color.

Once I was all set up and pleased with my profile, I decided to start browsing around. Clicking around on profiles, I discovered that the website required you to pay to send messages. You could wink at someone for free, but actually communicating meant spending real money. I got five free messages just for signing up, though, so I wanted to use them wisely. Most men under my stated preferences hadn't been logged in for a while, and even more had neglected to fill out their hobbies section, making it extremely difficult to judge who might make a good match. I was left to base it on looks alone. I scrolled through page after page, looking for the next devilishly handsome Mr. Right. At the end of a dozen pages, I'd sent out all five of my messages. *"Hello, my name is Anna. I'm an American, but I live in Jinan. I like to sing and read. Do you want to chat?"* I sent the same introduction to all five men, then decided to give it a rest for the night.

By the time I logged on again the next afternoon, two people had responded to my messages. The first was a Salar man.

"Hello, I'm Guo," he texted. *"Are you really American?"*

"Yes, I'm from Indiana," I typed into the response box, but when I tried to send, I was hit with an error message. Not enough credits to send messages. If I wanted to talk more, I'd have to spend money. I could send him a heart for free, though. So, I clicked the little "heart" icon, and off the emoji floated, fluttering into the ether. Then I moved on to the second man, a Manchurian.

His message was simple: his name, Du YeMing, followed by his WeChat number. He must have seen that I wasn't a paid member and known I couldn't respond. I was thankful for an alternate way to communicate. I added him as a WeChat contact.

He accepted almost immediately.

"*Hello, beautiful lady,*" he texted, a common greeting towards women.

"*Hello, handsome man, have you eaten?*" I responded, the latter phrase being a polite colloquialism.

"*No, I won't eat until I get off work in a few hours,*" he said, then asked, "*What's your name?*"

"*Anna,*" I told him, "*And yours?*"

"*Du YeMing,*" he said, "*but you can call me DuGe* (Brother Du). *Where in America are you from?*"

"*I'm from Indiana,*" I texted, then sent him a picture highlighting Indiana on the United States map. "*Are you from Qinghai?*"

"*I grew up in Qinghai, in the capital of Xining, but my parents are both from Harbin,*" he said. Then he continued, "*I'm half Han and half Manchurian. My family moved to Xining when I was 5 because my father was in charge of urban development here. Can you tell that I look different?*"

"*I can tell,*" I told him, and it was true. He was darker than most Han, with high cheekbones, broad eyes, and a narrow chin. "*I'm not any special ethnicity, I'm just white,*" I told him.

"*In China, that's a special ethnicity,*" he texted, sending along a laughing emoji.

We spent hours getting to know each other via text. DuGe was a 32-year-old professional driver, chauffeuring tourists around the Qinghai-Tibetan Plateau. Sometimes, he would be gone for days at a time. His longest tour lasted two weeks. At other times, he would be gone for just a few hours a day, taking people to and from Qinghai Lake. He said he enjoyed his job, and he found other people to be fascinating. But it didn't leave him much time to try and find a partner, at least not in the traditional dating sense. His ideal partner was someone who would either want to join him on his travels, or be okay with him being gone from the home for half the week. He would have plenty of time to chat whenever he wasn't driving, but he wouldn't be able to be online and available 24/7.

I was okay with all of that. I didn't care if he was home every night or not since I lived in a completely different province. When I told him this, he asked why I was looking for love in Qinghai instead of Jinan. I told him about my plans to move to Qinghai, and how the Plateau had stolen my heart. He said he completely understood, as he felt the same way. He told me he would show me all around the province next time I visited, and I told him I would remember his offer.

We exchanged photos of our families, divulged our dream careers, and discussed religion and politics. DuGe wasn't a fan of the Chinese Communist Party. He'd seen too many injustices done towards people of ethnic minorities, and he didn't feel like the government truly had the people's best interest in mind. He was an atheist, but didn't mind if others had religion. And he knew enough about Islam from growing up in a Muslim-majority city that he could even help me find resources once I got to the city.

The only negative thing about DuGe was that he was a chain smoker, and easily went through three packs of cigarettes a day. He swore he didn't stink, though. I believed him – strangely, despite the fondness for smoking in China, the smell of smoke didn't seem to linger on people, in cars, or in houses like it does elsewhere. Maybe we were all just blind to the scent. If smoking too much was the worst trait he had, I could probably look past it, especially since I was edging up to a pack a day myself.

By evening, I had decided that I liked DuGe well enough to

continue talking to him. He seemed genuinely interested in me as a person, not just the fact that I was a foreigner, although I'm sure that was part of the allure. Still, he held conversation well and we had similar interests and views on the world. I couldn't find any red flags on his social media, and I'd walked away from the conversation smiling. This was a good start.

I decided not to limit myself just to one person, though. There was no guarantee DuGe and I would even make it into a relationship, and there was no harm in talking to other people, right? So, I logged back on to Zhen Ai Wang and began scrolling through my matches again. Unable to send any more messages and unwilling to pay for a VIP membership, I spent the night clicking the little heart emoji next to the profiles I was most interested in.

I already had twenty-three new messages in my inbox, but they were all from people in Jinan, Beijing, or Shanghai, and most of the messages mentioned the word "foreigner". I deleted them all. I didn't particularly care that they were focusing on my foreign-ness, but if someone outside of my preference group was going to catch my eye, they were going to have to be much more creative than "hello, foreign beauty".

Only one other person responded to my heart emoji, though. He was a Hui man, short and very thin. His skin was light amber in color and his face was long and pointed. His profile picture showed him sporting a brown taqiyya and sky-blue jacket, standing in front of a picturesque rocky landscape. I found him to be incredibly handsome, and it looked like he enjoyed nature, which was a huge plus. He didn't have a VIP membership either, which meant the only thing he could do was respond to my heart by sending me a heart in return. You could only send one heart per day, however, so I returned his heart by sending another the next day. He followed suit. We continued on for three days like this before I had an idea.

I opened my profile picture with a photo editing app on my phone. Then I wrote the word "WeChat" followed by my username. I reuploaded the photo to Zhen Ai Wang and waited. A few hours later, my photo was removed from the website. I had broken the terms of service by adding personal information to my photo. So, I tried again, this time breaking up the characters for "We" and "Chat", and writing half of my username on one side of the photo and the other half on the opposite side. This one passed the verification test and stayed up.

Two days passed. We kept exchanging little hearts, but I received no request from him on WeChat. I was wondering if perhaps he didn't see my picture. I felt a little disappointed that my plan didn't work, but decided that on the next payday, I would pay for a VIP membership for just one month. That would let me send him my social media information, at least. But on day three, I was pleasantly surprised to wake up to a friend request from an unknown user in Xining, Qinghai. It was the Zhen Ai Wang guy! I eagerly accepted.

"*Hello!*" I texted. "*Are you from Zhen Ai Wang?*"

"*Yes, that's me!*" he responded. "*I saw your username in your photo. That was clever.*"

"*I was hoping you'd see,*" I said. "*I can't afford the VIP membership.*"

"*I can't either, but I was going to pay for a month next time I got my paycheck so I could message you!*" he said.

"*Haha, I was going to do the same,*" I told him. "*My name is Anna, what's yours?*"

"*My name is Ma JunHai,*" he said, but I pushed a little deeper.

"*That's your school name,*" I said. Hui people had several

names: the name their parents gave them at birth, the name their Imam gave them, and the name the school assigned them when they were officially assimilated into public schools and given a Mandarin name. *"What's your real name?"*

"WuMai," he responded, and then wrote, *"How did you know?"*

"I have a lot of Hui friends," I explained. I was part of a competitive karaoke group made up almost entirely of Hui people, and I'd had two Hui boyfriends in the past.

WuMai's name was the transliteration of Umar, and he was impressed that I knew so much about the Hui people. He was even more impressed when I told him about my conversion to Islam and my difficulty studying the prayers in Chinese.

"Allah looks most favorably upon those who try with all their heart and make mistakes, rather than those who can say the words perfectly but have empty hearts," he texted. *"I can help teach you, if you want."*

"Thank you," I said, *"I could certainly use more teachers."*

Getting to know WuMai, I learned that he was a driver for a Chinese meal delivery app, and spent his days speeding around Xining on his little yellow motorbike and matching yellow helmet. He was originally from Gansu, but his family moved to Xining when he was two years old. That meant he could speak *Putonghua*, or the standard Mandarin dialect, as well as *Qinghai Hua*, the Qinghai dialect, and *Gansu Hua*, the Gansu dialect, all of which were very different from each other. He was the third out of four boys in his family, and he loved exploring new places and adventuring outdoors.

"My parents used to own a restaurant, so I've cooked before, too," he said. *"And sometimes I use my brother's car to take tourists out to Qinghai Lake."* The majority of Qinghai's economy is built

on tourism.

I liked WuMai so far, but I wanted to be very clear with him about the type of person I was. I was practicing Islam now, sure, but I was being pretty lenient with the rules. *"You should know,"* I texted, *"that I smoke cigarettes and drink alcohol and I'm not a virgin."*

"That doesn't bother me," he responded. *"I used to smoke, but I quit. I've never had alcohol. And I'm not a virgin either. Do you wear your hijab when you smoke and drink?"*

"No, I take it off," I texted back. I'd been taught that was the respectful thing to do.

"That's good to hear," he said, and sent a wave of smiling emojis.

I found out that WuMai's birthday was 366 days before mine, that he loved kids and animals, and that he was fascinated by Japanese anime. He also liked sci-fi and fantasy themed movies, although he didn't care much for reading. He lived with his mother, father, two brothers and their wives, and a niece. His eldest brother lived away from home. (Ethnic minorities in China are allowed to have as many children as they'd like, unbeholden to the One Child Policy.)

We texted each other throughout the entire day, exchanging photos of what we were up to throughout the afternoon and asking questions about our families and day-to-day lives. Then I snuck in a big question, just to see if I should abandon the conversation early.

"How do you feel about gay people?" I asked. Most Chinese men that I knew were staunchly opposed and disgusted by the homosexual community, although most women didn't seem to care.

"I'm not gay, but I know a gay person," he said. *"It's not allowed*

in Islam, you know."

"I know, but do you think gay people should be banned from getting married?" I asked.

"I don't think they should have a Muslim wedding, but people should be free to do whatever they want. It doesn't hurt me if two gay people get married," he said.

I took this all as a positive sign. There were a number of people in my friends' group, both local and foreign, that were initially opposed to homosexual relationships, marriage, and the raising of children. But they all changed their minds when they discovered that some of the dear friends they'd grown close to in our little social group were, in fact, homosexual. WuMai was already expressing more tolerance than most would afford, and I was pretty certain that I could open his mind a bit more with time.

As the evening settled in, WuMai left the conversation to spend time with his family before heading to his mosque. Chatting with him had been like getting reacquainted with an old friend, and our talks had kept up a natural momentum. Still, we needed to leave more to talk about later, after the excitement of finding each other had worn off.

A short time later, DuGe messaged me.

"Good evening, Anna!" he wrote. *"I'm finally at my hotel. We drove to Black Horse River today."* Then he showed me his location on a map.

DuGe was eager to complain about his latest guests. They had complained about everything—the weather, the people, the food, the accommodations, even that he was driving too slowly. *"I'm exhausted,"* he said, *"and I have a feeling they're the type of people who are going to bother me in the middle of the night."*

"Does that happen a lot?" I asked.

"More than you might think," he said. *"But I get it from women more than men."*

"Really? What do the women want?" I asked.

"What do you think they want? You guess," he responded.

I knew what he was implying. *"Surely that's not true!"* I typed. *"You're just making that up."*

"No, I'm being serious!" he responded. *"It happens at least twice a month! And it's always in the middle of the night, and they're usually drunk."*

"Well, I guess that's a great perk of the job then," I said.

"Not really," he said, *"I never accept their offers. It's unprofessional, and I'm tired. All I want to do is eat and sleep, not fuck my customers."*

I was impressed by his stance, but perhaps that was a sign of his age. He had close to a decade on me, after all. He sent me a few photos of the scenic areas he'd traveled to that day, then told me he was ready for bed.

"I'm sorry I can't chat long," he texted, *"but I wanted to check in with you before I went to sleep. I was thinking about you all day."*

"You're very sweet," I told him. And then, *"I was thinking about you today, too."*

"Let's have a phone call next time, okay?" he suggested. I agreed, and we said goodnight.

That was the ritual for the rest of the week. I talked to WuMai during the day, and DuGe during the night. WuMai and I switched between texting and voice notes, but DuGe preferred talking over the phone. He said it was easier than typing, although it was harder for us to understand each other since I couldn't just translate the words I didn't know. He was patient with me, though, and was good about explaining what he meant when I couldn't make sense of it.

Even though I was talking with two men already, I kept my Zhen Ai Wang account active, and would occasionally scroll through my matches, just to see if anyone caught my eye. I sent a few more hearts to a few more men, but nothing ever came of it. A week later, a friend request appeared on my WeChat with the note "from Zhen Ai Wang" attached. At first I was curious as to how they found my WeChat number, until I remembered that I'd never swapped out the photo I uploaded for WuMai, and my username was still available for everyone to see. I accepted the request.

"Hello, I'm XiaoShi, I found you on Zhen Ai Wang," the message read.

"Hello, I'm Anna. Can you introduce yourself a bit?" I responded.

XiaoShi was a 27-year-old Hui man from Xining. He was well educated, studying to become a toxicologist. He sent me photos of the work he performed in his lab. He liked to read nonfiction books and listen to pop songs. XiaoShi was pudgy with a homely face, but seeing as I was the same, I didn't mind. I was more than willing to give him a chance beyond his looks, and it was clear very early that he was a highly intelligent individual. So, I began speaking with him daily too, although our conversations were sometimes lacking in excitement.

After a week of conversation, XiaoShi asked me why I had resorted to online dating when surely there were plenty of men in Jinan who would love a chance with a foreigner. I explained my reasoning to him, then asked him why he was using online dating, too. XiaoShi told me he had poor luck with women. He was married once before, but it didn't end well.

"Can I ask what happened?" I texted him.

"Well, I suppose you're going to find out one way or another,"

he responded.

I waited in anticipation for his answer.

"*I have a small penis,*" his message read, "*and I ejaculate prematurely. I could never satisfy her like she wanted, so she left me. But please don't let that make you hate me, I know how to use my hands and mouth, too, I promise. I can please a woman – all I ask for is patience.*"

I was shocked at his response. I certainly wasn't expecting that! Still, I appreciated his honesty and vulnerability. I could only imagine how nerve wracking it must be to divulge something like that to a stranger. I thought carefully about my response. Could I be okay with his situation?

"*Thank you for telling me that,*" I texted, "*and you're right, a penis isn't everything. There are many ways to please a woman. I don't mind being patient.*"

"*Thank you,*" he said, and then quickly moved on to another topic of conversation.

After two months of talking with my suitors, DuGe had started texting during the days, and WuMai's conversations would last until midnight. DuGe was mysterious and always on an adventure, WuMai was cheerful and hilarious, and XiaoShi was intelligent and sweet. I liked many things about all of them, but couldn't say I liked one more than the other, nor did I consider any of them to be my boyfriend. However, a week before Tomb Sweeping Day, WuMai had an idea.

"*Your work is closed for a few days for the holiday, right?*" he asked.

"*It is, we get all the major holidays off,*" I replied.

"*Well then why don't you come out to Xining for a visit?*" he suggested. "*I'll take you to see my favorite scenic areas and you can meet my family!*"

I liked the idea, and had enough funding to make it happen. This wouldn't be the first time I'd flown across the country by myself to meet a stranger.

"*Okay, I'll come,*" I responded.

"*Great!*" said WuMai. "*You can stay at my house.*"

"*I think I'd feel more comfortable in a hotel,*" I said. "*I'm not used to sleeping in stranger's houses.*"

"*That's okay,*" he replied. "*Whatever makes you feel the most comfortable.*"

And so, I purchased my plane tickets. I would leave early on a Friday morning and return to Jinan on Sunday afternoon. I decided to give myself enough time to potentially meet up with all three men, although I wasn't going to tell them specifics about each other. I told DuGe and XiaoShi that I was traveling to Xining to meet a friend, and would have some extra time if they wanted to get together. By that evening, a plan had been fully formed. On Friday at 10:00am, XiaoShi would meet me at my hotel. From there, he would take me on a day trip to visit Qinghai Lake, dropping me back off in Xining in time for DuGe to pick me up for dinner. Then I would spend all day Saturday with WuMai and eat dinner with his family. Then I would fly home on Sunday.

Three dates in two days. I was certainly planning on making good use of my time. When else was I going to have an opportunity to meet these men in person? The week seemed to drag by, although all of us were growing more excited by the day. Finally, Friday morning arrived, and I soon found myself on a plane headed west. Lucky for me, the airline had overbooked its economy seats, and since I was a single traveler, they upgraded my seat to first class. I sipped on a glass of red wine mixed with Sprite and leaned back deep in my seat, watching as the landscape below me changed from deep, lush greens to bright desert yellows.

My hotel was near the train station, closer to the city center than anything else. The city of Xining was laid out in an awkwardly angled X shape, and my hotel sat in what would be the lower right branch, as part of the old city. Xining was surrounded by mountains, and my hotel room had a view of the gently cascading northern slopes. The building was new, and the beds were soft. It was the best Super 8 I'd ever stayed in. Once I was settled in, I texted each of the men, letting them know I'd safely arrived. WuMai and DuGe were both busy with work, but XiaoShi said he was on the way to pick me up.

He knocked on my hotel room door at precisely 10:00am, just as he'd promised. He was all smiles, and he'd come with flowers. I invited him in.

"It's so good to finally meet you, Anna" he said, handing me the flowers. I placed them gently on the nightstand next to my bed.

"I'm so happy you're here," I told him. "I'm excited to see the lake!"

"Before we go, there's something I really want to ask you," he said, "and you can tell me no, I won't be upset, it's all up to you."

"What is it?" I asked curiously.

"M-m-may I k-kiss you?" he stuttered as he asked his question.

I smiled at him. "Sure," I said, "I don't mind a kiss."

XiaoShi stepped close to me and cupped my chin with one hand. Then he slid the other around my waist and pulled me close, kissing me deeply. He immediately opened his mouth, but his tongue was thick and sloppy. I didn't like the way it felt or tasted. I pulled back a bit, but XiaoShi held me tighter.

"That's enough," I said playfully, hoping he would stop.

But he grabbed at my breasts and tried to push me towards the bed. I pushed back against him, and XiaoShi took a step back before letting out a huge moan mixed with a whimper. Then he sat on the bed. It took me a minute to gather myself and realize what had happened. I was in a bit of panic mode from XiaoShi holding me and pushing me, fearing the worst. Then I noticed the wet spot on his pants, and I pieced together that he'd ejaculated after grabbing my breasts.

I took a step back towards the window as I watched XiaoShi begin to cry. His body shook as he let out a sob, then he turned to me, wiping his eyes.

"I'm so sorry," he said, "I didn't mean to. But I can make you feel good, I can use my hands, just let me try." He cried harder.

I felt bad for him, but I wanted him gone. I didn't feel safe with him. Still, I sat on the bed next to him and tried to console him.

"Things like this happen sometimes, it doesn't mean you're not a good person," I told him. I thought about giving him a reassuring touch on the back, but didn't want him to take it the wrong way. I was completely turned off by this man, and I was a little fearful that he was going to pressure me into doing things I didn't want to do with him. The last thing I wanted to do was spend the whole day with him.

"XiaoShi, my stomach hasn't been feeling well today," I told him, "I've had diarrhea since the plane. I think I'll be okay if I rest a bit, though. Do you think you could give me an hour?"

"Sure," XiaoShi said, "I can go get us some lunch. If you're still not feeling well by the time I get back, we can just watch a movie here."

With that, XiaoShi stood up and left my hotel room. I waited ten minutes after he left before sending him a text on WeChat.

"*I'm sorry, but I don't think we're compatible with each other. You are very nice, and the flowers are beautiful, but I think we should just be friends,*" I told him.

"*Okay, I understand,*" he responded. "*Will you still go to the lake with me?*"

"*No, I'm sorry,*" I texted back, "*I'm not ready to meet again.*"

That was the last I heard from XiaoShi. He removed me as a friend.

I didn't want to sit alone in my hotel room for the rest of the day, however. DuGe and I weren't planning to meet up until after 6pm, when he got back into town, so I had an entire afternoon. I decided to reach out to WuMai. I told him that my plans for that day didn't work out, and I was free until dinnertime. Did he know of any interesting places to see?

"*I know!*" he responded almost immediately. "*I'll take you! I know the perfect place! Give me an hour and I'll meet you at your hotel.*"

"*Don't you have to work?*" I asked.

"*Not if I don't want to,*" he responded. "*I just have to tell my boss I'm leaving.*"

An hour later, WuMai was at my door. He was both thinner and shorter than his pictures had led me to believe. He was barely an inch taller than me, although I wasn't bothered by height (or a lack thereof). His waist looked so small, I thought I could wrap my hands around him and still have my fingers touch. But he was dressed stylishly and wore a big, goofy grin that made me smile, too.

"I borrowed my brother's car and got us some snacks," he said. "I want to take you to see the Ta'Er Monastery."

I'd never been to a proper monastery before. Jinan had plenty of Confucian temples and smaller Buddhist temples around the city, but this would be my first time visiting a large compound. The drive through the southwestern arm of Xining took forty-five minutes, and we spent the entire time happily clucking away like hens. We chatted mostly about animals—our favorites and least favorites, animals in our hometowns, pets we had growing up, pets we'd like to have, animals we've ridden, animals we've eaten. The small talk was enough to keep us entertained.

The first thing I noticed about the monastery were the dozens of Tibetan men and women standing outside the walls, milling about but dressed in traditional Tibetan garb.

"There's a housing compound just for Tibetan people a block that way," WuMai explained, pointing with his chin. "The government paid for their apartments since they're an ethnic minority and poor. This makes it easier for them to live and find a good job." I wanted to probe more into his views on Tibet, but didn't think the monastery would be the appropriate time or place.

Despite being built in the 16th century, the monastery was robust and brightly colored. Red and yellow walls glowed as they showcased 400-year-old paintings. Rainbows of prayer flags were strung across the rafters of the main meditation hall. Old, iron bells chimed in the wind, and monks streamed in and out of buildings all across the compound. We spent a good three hours at the monastery, returning to the outside pavilion at the main entrance halfway through to snack on cumin-roasted tofu. Neither of us had eaten lunch.

"Thank you for showing me all of this," I said to WuMai at one point.

"It's nothing! There's a lot of culture in Xining," he said. "I'm Muslim, but I still appreciate the beauty of other people."

"I'm glad you think that way," I said.

My dinner date was still a few hours away when WuMai and I returned to my hotel, so I invited him into the room. As we sat on the bed, I logged into Facebook through my mobile VPN and showed him pictures of my hometown and my American friends. In turn, he showed me pictures from his hometown of Gansu and his school friends. He didn't have many photos on social media, explaining that the Hui aren't fond of posting photos of people online for strangers to see. Doing so was considered bad luck and harmful to the soul. A few minutes later, his phone rang. He answered in *Gansu Hua*. It was his brother, he said, wanting to know when he'd be home with the car. And so, he took his leave.

"I'll pick you up tomorrow at 9:30am, okay?" he said. "We have a lot to see!"

"Okay," I agreed as I walked him to the door. I'd had a very pleasant time with WuMai, and was excited to see what he had planned for the next day.

But I didn't have much time to think about it after he left – I still needed to get ready for dinner. I reached out to DuGe to confirm our plans were still on before taking a quick shower and changing my clothes. I'd gotten rather sweaty at the monastery and the wind had left a thin layer of dust on my outfit. It didn't take me long to freshen up, especially with my hair so short now.

"*I'm waiting for you in the lobby,*" DuGe texted shortly after 6:00pm.

I met him downstairs, and he escorted me to a black passenger van parked across the street.

"This is the car I use for the tourists," he said, opening the door for me.

The van was nice, and I told him as much. He thanked me, slid his keys into the ignition, then pulled out two cigarettes

– one for him, and one for me. Then he asked me about my day. I told him that my original plans were canceled, but luckily another friend had stepped in to rescue me from boredom and taken me to the monastery.

"The monastery is a great place to visit," DuGe said, lighting up his cigarette.

He wasn't very conversational, but I got the sense that he was tired. I spent just as much time looking out the window in silence as I did talking with him. By the time we stopped in front of the restaurant, he was on his third cigarette.

"My friend owns this place," he told me as he opened my car door and took my hand to help me out.

"It looks beautiful," I told him, admiring the carvings of sea monsters and pirate ships that spiraled around two wooden columns outside.

"The restaurant is pirate themed, but we're here for the barbeque and special drinks," he said, smiling.

Inside, the restaurant was completely empty, save for a middle-aged woman standing behind the counter. Her face lit up when she saw us.

"DuGe! Long time no see!" she exclaimed.

"Hi MeiMei," he said. "This is the friend I was telling you about. Her name is Anna."

"Hello, Anna!" MeiMei said cheerfully. "DuGe told me he wanted to treat you today. Welcome to my little restaurant!"

MeiMei led us to a table next to the far wall. She joined us as we took our seats, speaking to DuGe in *Qinghai Hua*. I couldn't understand a word they were saying, but they were smiling when their conversation ended. As MeiMei walked back towards the kitchen, I saw her look back over her shoulder and smile at me. I asked DuGe about all the driving he'd done that day, and he started to tell me about the places he'd visited and the group of four men he'd chauffeured around all afternoon.

MeiMei returned with a huge platter of barbeque skewers. There was cumin goat and garlic, chicken wings, pepper beef with charred fat pieces, and boiled edamame beans. MeiMei also set down a large, ornate glass in front of me. Dry ice flowed from the top, white smoke clashing with a blue liquid at the bottom. Then MeiMei pulled out a lighter and lit a small sparkler that I hadn't noticed before. The sparks from the firework danced across the plastic table as we ooh'd and aah'd. DuGe lit up another cigarette.

"This is my special drink," MeiMei said. "I made the formula myself. DuGe says it's the best drink in town."

"That's because it is!" DuGe exclaimed. "I would never tell a lie." He laughed and began turning a handful of barbeque skewers from the platter in my direction.

Our conversation over dinner was tense. I couldn't quite tell what it was, but it felt like DuGe was holding back. It seemed like he was analyzing me, his eyes attempting to pierce into me and see what I was made of. But he was extraordinarily kind and behaved like a gentleman. We talked about all the different countries we wanted to visit and what our dream homes would look like if money wasn't an issue. As we conversed, DuGe's shoulder length hair constantly fell into his eyes, adding to his look of mystery.

Dinner with DuGe was nice, but by the time we were done eating, I was still wanting more from him. I was already intellectually attracted to him, but something about his behavior tonight made me want him physically, too. When he drove me back to my hotel, I asked him to join me in my room. He agreed.

"I'm not sure I can be very respectful right now," he said as soon as the hotel room door was closed.

"I don't want you to be very respectful right now," I replied, and we both eagerly moved towards each other.

We locked in a passionate kiss as our hands found each other's bodies, tearing the clothes from one another as we made our way to the bed. He smelled sweet and tasted salty, and I could tell he was a man of experience. He had a number of surprising tricks to share, and the stamina to share them all.

He pulled me close to him as we lay on the bed, exhausted from the day.

"I wish I could stay all night like this," DuGe said, running his fingers through the tufts I called my hair, "but I have another group to take out tomorrow. I have to get up early."

"It's okay, I have plans tomorrow, too," I said.

"I know you have dinner plans tomorrow, but maybe we can meet up again afterwards. I want to see you one last time before you go," he said.

"I could probably make that work," I said. I wanted to see him again, too.

DuGe and I both smoked a cigarette before putting our clothes back on. I walked him to the hotel door, and we kissed goodnight. I decided to spend the rest of the night getting lost in TV shows, until a message from WuMai appeared on WeChat.

"*I'm so excited for tomorrow,*" the message read. "*What are you doing now?*"

We texted until 1:00am.

The next morning came all too soon, and when I saw WuMai outside of my hotel, I could tell he was just as tired as I was. That was the price we paid for not being able to put our phones down. We loaded up into WuMai's brother's car again and set off heading southwest out of the city. WuMai first took me to the peak of LaJi Mountain, where the snow was thick and the wind was cold. Colorful Tibetan prayer flags were strewn across the peak, indicating the holiness of the land. Then we traveled south to GuiDe and toured the vast geological site that boasted dozens of stone formations throughout the rainbow cliffs. WuMai knew just how much I loved geology, and was happy to indulge in my passions with me. Afterwards, we ended with dinner at his house. His mother had made goat and chive dumplings, one of the most delicious culinary experiences of my life. Perfectly tender and served with a garlic soy sauce, the juice wouldn't stop running down my chin after every bite. WuMai's mother was delighted that I enjoyed the food so much. At one point, while WuMai was in the bathroom, his mother sat down beside me on the couch.

"I like you," she said. "You can call me 'Mom'. I don't think this is the last time we'll see each other." She smiled at me, and I agreed to call her as she wished. She was a kind, portly old woman with a round face and cheeks that jutted out from her black lace hijab.

I had a great day with WuMai. He had impressed me with the trip to GuiDe and the mountain. We never ran out of things to talk about, and his family was both kind and generous. But my legs were exhausted from all the walking, and although I enjoyed my time with WuMai, I was ready for a break. He insisted he drive me back to my hotel, despite me assuring him that I could get a taxi with no problems. He wouldn't hear of it, though, saying there was no reason for me to spend my money when he was the one that took me to the other side of the city. Arriving at the hotel, he opened my car door to help me out.

"Can I give you a hug?" I asked, smiling.

"Sure!" he exclaimed, and hugged me tightly. "It was really great to meet you, Anna."

"It was great to meet you too, WuMai. We'll have to make sure this isn't the last time," I said.

"Maybe I can come to visit you in Jinan," WuMai suggested, and we agreed that should be our next plan.

Back at the hotel, I texted DuGe that I was ready for him to come over. He showed up with a bottle of wine, and we had an impassioned repeat of the previous night. This time, DuGe stayed the whole night, volunteering to take me to the airport the following day.

"Do you think you'll ever visit Jinan?" I asked him as we were lying in bed.

"Probably not," he said. "I'm busy almost all year round. I go back to my hometown in Harbin for the Spring Festival, though. Maybe you could come with me."

"I'd love to join," I said, wondering if he was serious. Then I melted in his arms and drifted off to sleep.

On the plane back to Jinan, I considered each of the three men that I'd met. My encounter with XiaoShi had left a sour taste in my mouth, and I didn't plan on seeking him out any further. What a relief he'd removed me from his contact list! Overall, I had the most fun with WuMai, who was the most open and cheerful. Spending time with WuMai felt like spending time with an old friend. But I'd enjoyed the mysterious aura around DuGe, too, and was eager to revisit our passionate nights. He didn't have as much free time, but he had the means to take me to incredible places. Neither man had been declared my boyfriend, and that was okay. I wanted a relationship something fierce, but was willing to take the time to get to know both of these people better before deciding on one or the other. Or perhaps neither.

Two months later, I found a job teaching English in Xining. It was an unexpected opportunity, but I jumped at the chance to leave Jinan before the summer officially started. WuMai traveled all the way out to Jinan to help me pack up my belongings and get them on a truck. Then he packed my cats and I up, too, and hired a car to drive us the entire distance back to Xining. Both DuGe and WuMai were happy to show me around the city, and I spent time with each of them as equally as I could. Neither knew about the other, however, and by the time WuMai asked me to be his girlfriend, DuGe and I had begun to discover several points of incompatibility between us.

DuGe and I remain friends, though the light has left his eyes. He contracted Buerger's disease from the excessive smoking, causing his legs to become riddled with gangrene and eventually amputated in 2018. With no legs, he stays confined to a bed, too ill and depressed to venture further from the house he now shares with his mother. He hopes to one day be able to afford a nice wheelchair, and maybe if he's really lucky, some prosthetic legs. He misses adventuring into the wilds of Qinghai every day. I never knew what became of XiaoShi, but I hope he found someone who could give him more patience than I could.

In the end, I married WuMai, much to his mother's delight. When I found out I was pregnant, I returned to the United States. WuMai did not follow, however, instead insisting that I return to China with the baby, and go back to teaching English while he took over childcare duties. This led to our divorce three years later. The divorce was only religious, however, as we still remain legally married in the eyes of Chinese laws. As far as WuMai is concerned, he's free to take another wife, but they can only be married ceremoniously. He swears to this day he'll never marry again. WuMai doesn't have much contact with his daughter, but his mother and I talk almost daily. After we divorced, I left Islam, although I kept most of the headscarves, souvenirs of a life I lived so passionately.

Although I left China at the age of twenty-five, China has never left me. My heart speaks a tonal language while it bleeds American blood. Having a daughter who is half-Chinese, the country is a daily topic of conversation, and in a few years, maybe she, too, will find herself on a plane headed east, determined to discover herself, eager for adventure, starving to devour a little bit more of the world. As for myself, I don't feel like I've ever truly integrated back into American culture. There's just something that feels... missing. A small void that remains to be filled. A deep sense of longing. An emotion that flares wildly, yet remains unnamed. I don't shy away from this feeling, though. Rather it guides me as I take the hands of my children and walk with them through the quest of living life with fervor, curiosity, and compassion.

About the Author

Anna Keibler is a disabled, neurodivergent LGBTQ+ professional writer, youth worker, and traveler with a fervent passion for languages, art, and wildlife. As a nature lover with a master's  in natural resources, she has a passion for the ecological conservation of the Qinghai-Tibetan Plateau.

Originally hailing from rural Indiana, Anna learned Mandarin after living and working in China for more than five years. With more than a decade of experience in teaching English, essay writing, and research strategies, she has built a strong foundation of creative writing experience in the nonfiction space. Her first book, *A Ghost in the Middle Kingdom*, was published in 2025.

In her spare time, Anna can often be found crafting, adventuring, enjoying Chinese folk music, and scouring either the night sky for unusual astral phenomena or her backyard for natural herbal remedies.

Apprentice
House Press
Loyola University Maryland

Apprentice House Press is the country's only campus-based, student-staffed book publishing company. Directed by professors and industry professionals, it is a nonprofit activity of the Communication Department at Loyola University Maryland.

Using state-of-the-art technology and an experiential learning model of education, Apprentice House publishes books in untraditional ways. This dual responsibility as publishers and educators creates an unprecedented collaborative environment among faculty and students, while teaching tomorrow's editors, designers, and marketers.

Eclectic and provocative, Apprentice House titles intend to entertain as well as spark dialogue on a variety of topics. Financial contributions to sustain the press's work are welcomed. Contributions are tax deductible to the fullest extent allowed by the IRS.

To learn more about Apprentice House books or to obtain submission guidelines, please visit www.apprenticehouse.com.

Apprentice House Press
Communication Department
Loyola University Maryland
4501 N. Charles Street
Baltimore, MD 21210
Ph: 410-617-5265
info@apprenticehouse.com • www.apprenticehouse.com